LORD WILLIAM BENTINCK

LORD WILLIAM BENTINCK

DEMETRIUS C. BOULGER

GYAN

Published by

Gyan Publishing House
5, Ansari Road
Daryaganj, New Delhi-110002
Phone: 011-47034999, 9811692060
E-mail: books@gyanbooks.com

Distribution Network
gyanbooks.com
India, USA, Canada, UK, Australia, France

ISBN : 978-81-212-9524-6 (PB)
First Published, 1892

2nd Impression 2023

Printed at: Gyan Press, Delhi.

LORD WILLIAM BENTINCK
Author: DEMETRIUS C. BOULGER

RULERS OF INDIA

EDITED BY

SIR WILLIAM WILSON HUNTER

HENRY FROWDE, M.A.
PUBLISHER TO THE UNIVERSITY OF OXFORD
LONDON, EDINBURGH, NEW YORK
TORONTO AND MELBOURNE

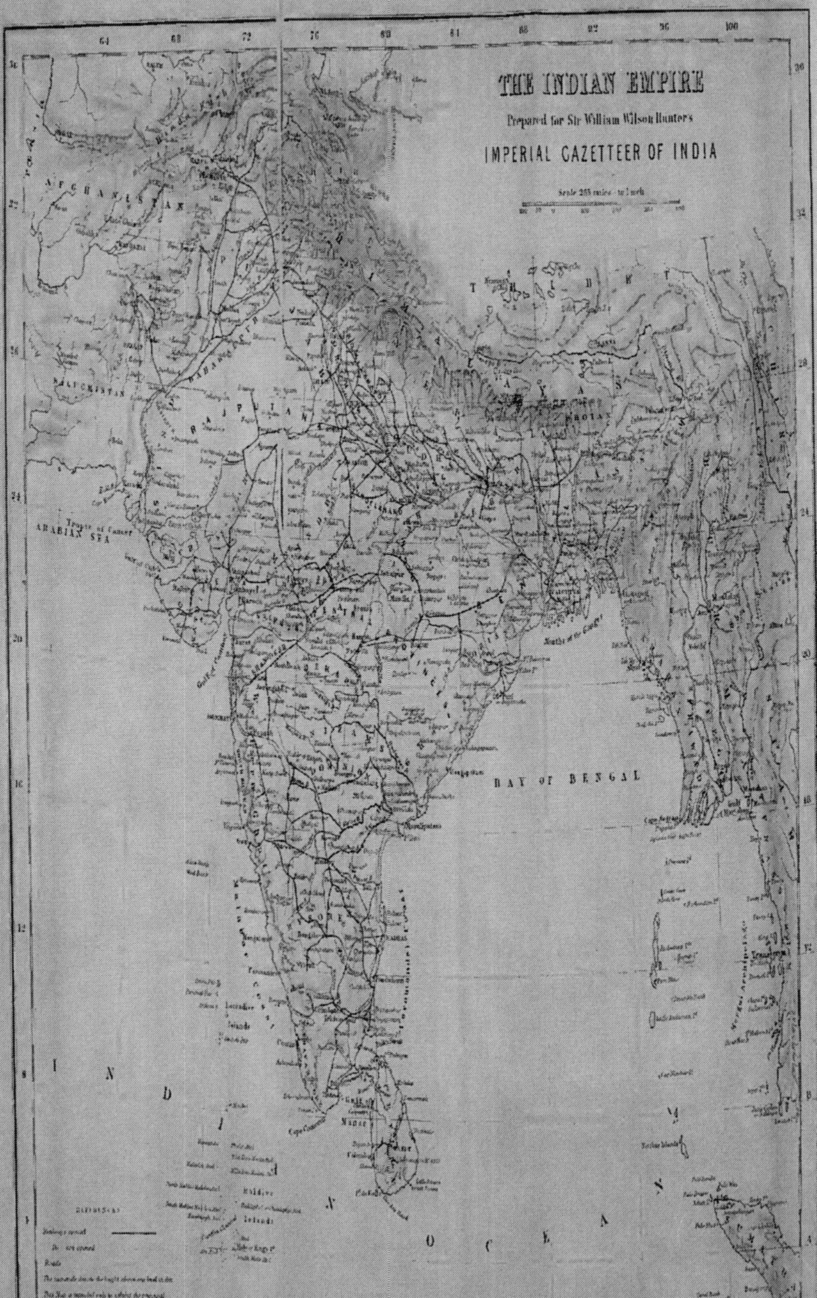
THE INDIAN EMPIRE
Prepared for Sir William Wilson Hunter's
IMPERIAL GAZETTEER OF INDIA
AFGHANISTAN
BALUCHISTAN
RAJPUTANA
TIBET
ARABIAN SEA
Tropic of Cancer
BAY OF BENGAL
Mouths of the Ganges
I N D I A N O C E A N
Long. E. of Greenwich

LORD WILLIAM BENTINCK

BY

DEMETRIUS C. BOULGER

MDCCCXCVII

CONTENTS

NOTE

The orthography of proper names follows the system adopted by the Indian Government for the *Imperial Gazetteer of India.* That system, while adhering to the popular spelling of very well-known places, such as Punjab, Lucknow, &c., employs in all other cases the vowels with the following uniform sounds:—

a, as in wom*a*n: *á*, as in f*a*thers: *í*, as in pol*i*ce *i*, as in intr*i*gue: *o*, as in c*o*ld: *u*, as in b*u*ll: *ú*, as in s*u*re: *e*, as in gr*e*y.

LORD WILLIAM BENTINCK

CHAPTER I

EARLY LIFE

THE administration of Lord William Bentinck was one of peace. Following the administrations of Cornwallis, Wellesley, Hastings, and Amherst, and preceding those of Auckland, Hardinge, and Dalhousie, through the absence of foreign adventure and territorial conquest his Governor-Generalship may seem commonplace in comparison with conquerors who crushed the Mysore and Maráthá confederacies, planted the banners of the Company on the Indus and the Irrawaddy, and put forward the right of the rulers of India to exercise a controlling influence over Afghánistán. But the very contrast between the character of Lord William Bentinck's administration and that of the other British Governor-Generals whom we have named serves to bring into stronger relief the importance of the work he accomplished in the making of the India of to-day.

The youngest student of the growth of the British power in India does not need to be told that we first went to that country as traders, and that our only representatives were merchants who thought nothing about the politics of the country or of interfering with the Native Powers, and who were exclusively engaged in their counting-houses. That condition of things went on for nearly 150 years, and when the competition with the French, who would have expelled all other European traders if the programme of Dupleix had been realised, resulted in our unexpected triumph, accomplished by the genius of Clive, the East India Company—still cherishing above territorial possessions and military glory the commercial monopoly granted by Elizabeth and extended by Anne—preserved its character as a society of merchants, esteeming its annual investment in country goods, whether in Bengal, Bombay, or Madras, of far higher importance than matters of administration.

The East India Company, true to its origin, clung to its pacific vocation to the end, in spite of every temptation to play a sovereign part. Greatness was forced upon it by the many remarkable men who appeared in its service for sixty years after Clive had pointed out the easy and attractive road to wider dominion. It regretted the diversion of money from the legitimate pursuit of trade to the maintenance of armies, and it only reconciled itself to the course because Warren Hastings proved that the execution of a great policy in India did not necessarily entail the payment of a smaller dividend in Leadenhall Street. The conquest of a fresh province was for many years the cause of as much anxiety as satisfaction to the Honourable Court.

When the Charter of the East India Company was renewed by Parliament in 1793 those feelings were in full force, and if it had then been renewed with any serious diminution of its commercial privileges it would have been deprived of half its value. Very much the same feeling was prevalent when it was again renewed in 1813, although on this occasion the Company was deprived of the monopoly of the trade with India. It retained however the most favoured position for carrying on this trade, and it preserved the monopoly of that with China. Lord William Bentinck was sent to India when the renewal of the Charter had again become imminent and formed the burning question in Anglo-Indian circles, but a great change had passed over the spirit of the Directors of the East India Company. Certain facts had become patent to even the most prejudiced minds in Leadenhall Street, and it was recognised that a change was at hand. The maintenance of any commercial monopoly was in antipathy to the free spirit of a trading people like the English. That certain gentlemen trading with China should be privileged, and that the bulk of the nation attempting the same thing should be denounced as interlopers, outside the law, and little better than pirates, was nothing more or less than an anachronism. The Court had begun to realise in 1827, when it offered the Governor-Generalship to Lord William Bentinck, that a radical change in its tenure of authority in India was at hand, and that its career might be curtailed if not summarily ended.

There was no longer any reasonable hope of its retaining an exclusive hold upon China, and as its connection with that country was purely commercial, and as it possessed no territorial base to put it on terms of vantage with outside traders, the withdrawal of the monopoly could not but signify a distinct loss of revenue. This prospect was rendered the more serious because the profits from the Chinese trade were far in excess of its dimensions, and because the capacity of the Chinese for consuming opium and paying silver then seemed to be unlimited. At the same moment it happened that the heavy expenses of the first Burmese war had produced a serious deficit in the finances of India, which inspired apprehension for the future. The possible loss of any source of revenue or profit was therefore a cause of the deepest solicitude to the Court, and it consequently became a matter of the first importance to ascertain how far an equilibrium in the finances could be attained by internal economies and a rigid abstention from external adventures. The solution of that difficult problem was entrusted to Lord William Bentinck, and it remains to his enduring credit that he solved it with perfect satisfaction to his employers and to the natives of India.

The withdrawal of its last trading monopoly and the cessation of its commercial character brought the East India Company face to face with grave administrative responsibilities. It is quite true that it had already accepted and accomplished the task of governing India; but to govern India under the conditions which prevailed when Clive, Warren Hastings, or even Wellesley, ruled supreme, was less difficult than it had become in Bentinck's day or than it is now. In the earlier days public opinion was rarely aroused in Indian matters except to applaud the result, and as the result was always a triumph searching criticism was never called forth. But in these times, and the origin of the method dates from the rule of Lord William Bentinck, every act or measure of the Indian Executive is subjected to the severest and most searching criticism long before it is possible to say what its result will be. During the debates on the renewal of the Charter there were the loudest protestations on both sides that India would suffer if the decision of matters affecting it were to be biassed by the party considerations prevailing in English politics.

The acceptance of the Government of India by the East India Company in 1833 in the most formal manner as the delegate of the British Crown and Parliament, and the recognition of its responsibility for the charge to the House of Commons and public opinion, was a grave and momentous step, as the Company did not possess the machinery necessary to discharge its trust with efficiency and with satisfaction to the public conscience. It is true that the cessation of their duties as merchants left the servants of the Company at liberty to devote their time and attention to matters of administration and affairs of State. But their numbers were not sufficient, and the revenue would not admit of their increase, to enable the Indian Government to perform all the duties that were expected of it. The solution of these difficult questions was not found during Lord William Bentinck's administration alone, but he certainly indicated the true direction in which they should be solved, and provided to a great extent the machinery for solving them. The part which Lord William Bentinck took in abolishing certain malpractices and inhumanities deserves a tribute of praise, and will be referred to in its proper place; but the momentous decision to make the English language the official and literary tongue of the Peninsula represents the salient feature in his administration, and makes his Governor-Generalship stand out as a landmark in Indian history.

His tenure of authority thus represents a turning-point in British rule in India. It includes the period when the East India Company, casting aside its garb as a commercial body, boldly grappled with Indian problems, and became a reigning Government alone. The essential difference in the principle of administration was well described by the late Sir Charles Trevelyan in his evidence before the Select Committee of 1853:—

'To Lord William Bentinck belongs the great praise of having placed our dominion in India on its proper foundation in the recognition of the great principle that India is to be governed for the benefit of the Indians, and that the advantages which we derive from it should only be such as are incidental to and inferential from that course of proceeding.'

Regarded from a true historical standpoint there is no period in the British rule of India which deserves more attentive study than that which witnessed the disappearance of the old trading Company that had originally been started for the exploration of the Indies more than two centuries before, and the formal assumption by the Company of the heavy task of governing the millions of India, as the delegate of the British Crown and Parliament, with absolute justice, impartiality, and efficiency. It is chiefly with regard to this historical metamorphosis that I am about to attempt to bring out the salient features in the life and Governor-Generalship of Lord William Bentinck. The biographical details of his career, although interesting and varied, must be held subordinate to the part that he played in the development of the British administration of India.

The family of Bentinck, which has occupied in English politics and society a prominent and honourable position during the last two centuries, ranks among the noblest in the Netherlands. The head of the family still resides on the patrimonial property in the province of Overijssel and employs the style of Count, a title conferred on his ancestors in the most flourishing days of the Holy Roman Empire. But the greater splendour and wealth of the younger branch, which came to England in the person of Hans William Bentinck in the train of William of Orange, has eclipsed the origin from which it sprang, and the historical interest centres in the Dukes of Portland and not in the Counts Bentinck. Macaulay has described in his brilliant manner the friendship of William of Orange and Bentinck, the growth of Bentinck's fortunes after his master became King of England, and how, notwithstanding the bitter opposition of the English Parliament, which went so far as to impeach him, Bentinck retained the large estates in England, Wales, and Ireland, and the title of Earl of Portland, conferred on him by his grateful and much attached sovereign. Having passed successfully through the ordeal which was inevitable before even the most favoured Dutch nobleman could be allowed by insular prejudice to take a prominent place in the House of Peers, the Earl of Portland lost no opportunity of ingratiating himself and his family with English opinion and qualifying himself for the requirements of our country life. He had married an English lady long before there appeared any chance of his settling in England. His son (the first Duke of Portland) and his grandson followed his example by marrying into the noble families of Gainsborough and Oxford.

In the next generation it was almost forgotten that the Bentinck family was one of the few remaining evidences that a Dutch King had reigned over the United Kingdom. The third Duke married Lady Dorothy Cavendish, the only daughter of the fourth Duke of Devonshire, who had played a considerable part in politics during the reign of George the Second and the earlier years of his successor. By this alliance the Dukes of Portland became connected with the most ancient and distinguished families of the kingdom, and from that time to the present their family has been known by the double name of Cavendish-Bentinck. In 1783 the Duke of Portland, more by the exigencies of party and for the sake of his spotless character than for exceptional ability, was promoted to the Prime Ministership, but the events of his administration were unimportant, and perhaps the most interesting fact about his public career was that he was one of the persons supposed to have been Junius. But for us he has a more personal interest in that he was the father of Lord William Bentinck.

William Cavendish-Bentinck, second son of the third Duke of Portland, was born on 14th September, 1774. In 1791 he entered the Coldstream Guards as an ensign, and in the following year he obtained his captaincy in the 2nd Light Dragoons. Two years later he had attained the rank of Lieutenant-Colonel of the 24th Light Dragoons, and in the campaign in Flanders of 1794, which was not creditable to the English arms, he served on the staff of the Duke of York. His zeal for the service was shown by his personal request, made through his father, to serve in the West Indies while the troops remained in quarters during the winter of 1793–4.

From one or two passing references, and from the fact that he was mentioned in despatches, we may assume that this youthful colonel and aide-de-camp of twenty showed that he possessed some soldierly qualities. Four years later he was specially selected for the honourable and responsible task of accompanying the army of Marshal Suwarrow in its campaign in Northern Italy and Switzerland as the military representative of England. During the campaign of 1799 he acquired a practical experience of the larger operations of war such as was not possessed by many other English officers at that time. After Suwarrow withdrew from Switzerland he remained in the same capacity with the Austrian army[1] in the north of Italy until the end of 1801. He was present at the decisive battle of Marengo, which established the reputation of Napoleon as one of the greatest military geniuses that the world had ever seen, and throughout the whole of the Italian campaign of 1800–1 he was always to be found wherever the severest fighting was in progress. It is only needful to name the engagements at which he was present. Besides Marengo, he saw, and wrote the official account for the English Government of, the battles of the Trebbia, Novi, Sangliano, and the

[1] In one of his despatches he bore eloquent testimony to the valour and devotion of the Austrian army, which has found far too few to appreciate it. 'It is impossible to do justice to the valour and perseverance of the Austrian army,' he wrote.

passages of the Mincio and Adige. He also witnessed the sieges of Alessandria and Coni. Although still quite young, he had had six or seven years' experience of the extensive warfare going on in Europe, and had seen Continental armies as well as English troops engaged with the French. He had also acquired some practical knowledge of the political condition and popular feelings of Northern Italy—a fact which explained his action many years later, when he exercised authority in Sicily and appeared as a victor at Genoa.

From Italy he proceeded to Egypt, where he had been appointed to command the cavalry attached to the force under Sir R. Abercromby, but he arrived too late to take an active part in the war, and the Treaty of Amiens giving brief tranquillity to Europe, Lord William Bentinck was relieved of his duties and returned to England. Very shortly after his return he married on February 19, 1803, Lady Mary Acheson, second daughter of the first Earl of Gosford. Three months after his marriage he was nominated by the East India Company to the Governorship of its Presidency at Fort St. George, Madras; and thus, as perhaps the youngest Governor ever sent from these shores to rule an Eastern dependency, he commenced that Indian career which twenty-five years later was to be renewed in a loftier position and with wider responsibilities. The Court was probably influenced in making the appointment by the exceptional military experience of Lord William Bentinck, and by the consideration that French designs upon India raised ever recurring alarms until after the retreat from Moscow. Support is lent to this opinion by the fact that during his Governorship the defence of the coast of Coromandel and of Ceylon against a French descent formed subjects to which he very frequently drew attention. His tenure of power at Madras introduced him at an early age to Indian responsibilities and difficulties, and his experiences there—which were, as will be seen, not free from bitterness—exercised a marked influence on his subsequent character and career.

CHAPTER II

THE GOVERNORSHIP OF MADRAS

LORD WILLIAM BENTINCK reached Madras on August 30, 1803, succeeding in the post of Governor of Fort St. George Lord Clive, the only son of the conqueror of Bengal. Important as this office still was, the centre of English power had been finally shifted from the coast of Coromandel to the valley of the Ganges by the break-up of the Muhammadan dynasty of Mysore, and the questions with which Lord William Bentinck was required to deal were mainly of local interest. Had he reached India only five years earlier he would have had an opportunity of displaying his energy and military talent in the closing scenes of Tipú's remarkable career, but although we were engaged during the period of his Governorship in a keen struggle with the Maráthás in the Deccan and Central India, he took only a subsidiary part in the campaigns which placed Lake and Arthur Wellesley in the first rank of Anglo-Indian commanders. The field of action was too far removed from Madras for that Presidency to take the leading part against Holkar as it had done against Haidar and Tipú. Lord William Bentinck was able to render Sir Arthur Wellesley useful assistance in regard to supplies, and his co-operation received official recognition and the expression of gratitude from both the commander in the field and the Governor-General.

The Governor-General of Fort William in Bengal was then the Marquis Wellesley, one of the ablest and most successful of the British statesmen who have ruled India. When Lord William Bentinck arrived in India the Marquis Wellesley was at the height of his fame, and it may be doubted if any Governor-General ever inspired his subordinates with so much admiration and enthusiasm as he did. He at once sent Colonel Hoghton, a trusted and confidential officer 'belonging to my family,' to quote the words of the Marquis, to meet the new Governor of Madras on his arrival, and to acquaint him with the exact position of affairs in India, and with the objects of his policy. The first letter Lord William Bentinck addressed to the Marquis Wellesley ten days after his arrival in India, and on Colonel Hoghton's return to Calcutta, is dated September 9, 1803. He says:—

'I am quite aware of the arduous and important task which I have undertaken. The divided state of this government, and the opposition and counteraction which my noble predecessor received, are circumstances much to be lamented, and which tend to destroy all the vigour and efficiency so imperiously required in the management of this great unsettled territory.'

He declared 'a steady and determined resolution to do what is right, uninfluenced by party or prejudice, careless and fearless of the result.'

The Marquis Wellesley seems to have been pleased with the language of his new colleague, from whom he looked for efficient co-operation in the large schemes engaging his attention, and also for a speedy solution of the difficulties besetting the administration of Fort St. George. He presently sent another officer (Captain Sydenham) to Lord William Bentinck, and dwelt in his despatch of November 19, 1803, on 'the truly British spirit, sound judgment, and hereditary integrity and honour' shown in the letter we have quoted.

The Governor-General in the following year called attention to what he considered a spirit of faction as being prevalent at Madras, and he also seemed to express some dissatisfaction with Lord William Bentinck's mode of dealing with it. Lord William replied admitting that such a state of things did undoubtedly exist, but that 'it was confined to a very few individuals and deserving of the most sovereign contempt.' At the same time he firmly but courteously upheld his right as an independent Governor to deal with such matters in his own way and on his own responsibility. In the relations of these two remarkable men it is more gratifying to turn to the agreeable features than to dwell on the one discordant note which revealed itself. The general admiration of the Anglo-Indian community for Lord Wellesley found expression in addresses presented from all parts of India in the spring of 1804. The Madras address was sent in May, 1804, under a covering letter from Lord William

Bentinck, which provided him with the opportunity of stating his views on the subject of Indian government,—views to which he was himself to give effect thirty years later.

'It is most pleasing to reflect that the result of the war affords a hope of equal benefit to the great mass of the people whose rulers have been conquered. If the annals of Indian history are retraced, and more particularly the events of later years, it will be found that this vast peninsula has presented one continual scene of anarchy and misery. Constant revolutions, without even a proposed legitimate object, have succeeded each other. Wars of great and petty chieftains, unwarranted in their origin and unprincipled in their conduct, for the sole object of robbery and plunder, have depopulated and laid waste the general face of this unhappy country. Justice, order, consideration of public and private rights nowhere appear in relief of this melancholy picture. Happily a period has arrived to these barbarous excesses. For the first time the blessings of universal tranquillity may be expected. That system of policy which could embrace the whole of India, which could comprehend in one bond of mutual defence and reciprocal forbearance the predatory chiefs of this great Empire, deserves the admiration of all the civilised world. That system, one of the noblest efforts of the wisdom and patriotism of a subject, which has founded British Greatness upon Indian Happiness, demands in a particular manner the thanks and applause of his country.'

These sentiments would have been praiseworthy from any one at a time when little or no heed was given to the obligations imposed upon us by the gradually extending conquest of India, but coming as they did from a young man who had not completed his thirtieth year, and whose acquaintance with India had only just commenced, they cannot but be considered as remarkable evidence of independence of character and breadth of view. They show beyond dispute that Lord William Bentinck held clearly defined opinions upon our position in India from the time that he first became connected with it, and that, as he put it, he considered British greatness should be founded on Indian happiness.

Although the great struggle for supremacy in Southern India was over before Lord William Bentinck reached Madras, there was still some anxiety prevalent as to the possible return of the French. French privateers continued to haunt the Indian seas, and although Pondicherry was in our possession, French spies and agents were believed to keep up communications with the native Courts and to send information to France viâ the Mauritius. Lord William Bentinck's anxiety was increased by the decline in the military strength and efficiency of the Madras army owing to the withdrawal of the Bombay troops, and this weakening of the garrison was the more calculated to stimulate alarm because both at Calcutta and at Madras there was a real fear that the French might attempt a descent either on Ceylon or on the coast of Coromandel. Lord William Bentinck thought such a descent perfectly feasible and easy in the case of Ceylon, which he described as 'unprotected without and within.' The threatened danger, however, passed off; and the French invasion only gave rise to the trial of M. Collin, a resident at Pondicherry, and described as a man of ability, on a charge of being a secret agent and spy of the French Government.

No opportunity of giving effect to his political views presented itself during Bentinck's stay at Madras. Internal questions aroused little or no interest except when they referred to the policy of native states or the attitude of the leading chiefs. One of his most important acts related to the prohibition against any European travelling more than fifteen miles from the city of Madras without a passport, and specified the officials with whom the power of issuing such passports lay. This measure was intended as much as a precaution against French agents as for the maintenance of the Company's commercial rights. The land question was the pressing economic subject that presented itself during this period, and Lord William Bentinck was content with regard to it to adopt the opinions of Sir Thomas Munro. In Bengal Lord Cornwallis, when deciding the questions of land tenure and land revenue, had given a 'permanent settlement' and had established, or at least recognised, and strengthened by so doing, the class of the zamindárs or landlords. In Madras, where the same problem had to be met and solved only a few years later, exactly the opposite policy was pursued, and mainly owing to the efforts of Sir Thomas Munro. There we gave no indefeasible rights of tenure, and we recognised as the class identified with the soil not the zamindárs, but the cultivators. In Lord William Bentinck's opinion—'it was apparent to him that the creation of zemindars, where no zemindars before existed, was neither calculated to improve the condition of the lower orders of the people, nor politically wise with reference to the future security of this Government.'

Reference has been made to the bickerings and spirit of faction displayed at Madras. The correspondence of Lord William Bentinck, which has been discovered after lying for many years in obscurity, contains abundant evidence on the subject, and the discussions between the Governor on the one side and the Chief Justice (Sir Henry Gwillim) and members of the Governor's Council on the other, may be described as scarcely less heated than those that took place thirty years before at the Council-board of Warren Hastings. If there was no duel to compare with that between Hastings and Francis, we have a point blank refusal from the highest judicial authority to accept an invitation to Government House, and the highest administrative authority declining to hold any direct communication with the first of the Judges.

The difference of opinion between Lord William Bentinck and Sir Henry Gwillim seems to have had its origin in a very trifling matter. A native left a sum of money for a local charity, and the Government had to decide what was the best mode of dealing with the trust. Sir Henry Gwillim was consulted and made certain suggestions for its disposal. The matter seems to have lain dormant, or to have passed from Lord William Bentinck's memory for twelve months, and then to have been brought under his notice with a definite scheme for dealing with it as a fresh matter by some subordinate official. In ignorance of the character of the man with whom he had to deal, Lord William wrote to Sir Henry Gwillim asking him his opinion on this project, and stating at the same time that it had his complete approval.

The scheme varied in some respects from that recommended by Sir Henry twelve months before, and he at once interpreted Lord William's letter as an intended snub, and replied in terms of great asperity. Lord William Bentinck seems to have completely forgotten the earlier expression of opinion by the Chief Justice, or to have considered that no definite propositions had been put forward for dealing with the trust until that upon which he requested the opinion of Sir Henry Gwillim. The further correspondence, which ought to have explained away the difference, was marked by increased bitterness, and an attempt to effect an amicable understanding through an intermediary, Mr. A. Anstruther, member of Council, only resulted in aggravating the feeling of bitterness on both sides. On the one hand, Lord William Bentinck 'declined all further correspondence unless I am addressed in the language of polished intercourse, rather than in that of judicial rebuke,' and described Sir Henry's character to a common friend in the following words—'Sir Henry has something of the constitutional agitation of Holkar. He likes to make war upon his neighbours, not for the purpose of stealing their purse, but without an equally innocent intention against their good name.' On the other hand, Sir Henry Gwillim delivered an address to the Grand Jury which breathed defiance and hostility to the Governor, and he refused all invitations to Government House. Both however agreed on the main point that the custody of the funds should remain with the Court.

Lord William Bentinck's relations with several members of his Council were also strained. In 1806 he had felt compelled, for reasons which appeared to him convincing, and which there is every ground for believing were excellent, to appoint Mr. Robert Strange member of Council, and to pass over Mr. Thomas Oakes, who held the senior claim. The matter was referred to London for ratification, but the Court overruled Lord William Bentinck's decision, repudiated the appointment of Mr. Strange, and nominated Mr. Oakes to the seat. As Mr. Oakes had been opposed to Lord William Bentinck, this measure was of a character that he could not but resent, and in a letter to his brother Lord Titchfield, he declared his intention of resigning if the Court did not cancel its orders on the subject. His natural indignation seems to have been mollified by the Court's having exacted some personal promise from Mr. Oakes that he would not encourage any factious opposition to Lord William, or display any personal hostility. This promise was not better kept than such promises ever are, and Mr. Oakes showed himself not less hostile in the council-chamber than Sir Henry Gwillim on the bench.

It is curious to discover that at the very moment when Lord William Bentinck had the best reason to believe that the Court would not support his legitimate authority, and that he might feel it incumbent upon him to resign, there was a possibility of his being elevated to the higher office of Governor-General. This statement is made on the unimpeachable authority of the President of the Board of Control. In a letter to Lord William Bentinck, Lord Minto explained that the Government had nominated the Earl of Lauderdale as successor to the Marquis Cornwallis, and that the Court had absolutely refused to endorse the nomination. The Government did not relish the unqualified rejection of its nominee, but the Court declared its intention to stand firm even to the jeopardy of its Charter. In such conflicts a compromise provides the only remedy, and the transfer of Lord William Bentinck from Fort St. George to Fort William was seriously considered as the best arrangement. As a matter of fact it was not carried out, for the acting Governor-General, Sir George Barlow, was confirmed in his office. But the incident throws a significant side-light on the strangely conflicting views that must have been held in Leadenhall Street about the merit of Lord William Bentinck[1].

But the most important and memorable event in connection with Lord William Bentinck's Governorship of Madras was that which brought it to a sudden and disagreeable termination—the Mutiny at Vellore. The circumstances relating to this occurrence claim more than passing notice, both from a historical and a biographical point of view. They refer to one of the most remarkable crises in our military history in India before the Mutiny, and they unquestionably exercised a considerable influence on the Indian career and character of Lord William Bentinck.

Vellore, at all times a considerable military station, lies west of the city of Madras, and not far distant from Arcot, where Clive first revealed his military genius. It had become of increased importance by having been chosen as the place of residence for the family of the famous Tipú Sultán. The sons of that

[1] As evidence bearing on Lord William Bentinck's footing with the East India Company the following passage from a letter from Viscount Castlereagh, dated 8 November, 1805, may be quoted: 'I have much pleasure in finding a disposition in Leadenhall Street very favourably to consider your Lordship's measures. They are impressed with your determination to act for yourself, to conduct the public business in its accustomed channels, and to treat them with respect. Every man in public life must expect Rubs, more particularly when acting under a body so constituted.' Lord William Bentinck's own opinion was given in a letter based on this communication: 'It is not easy for me to give credit to this assurance, however anxious I may be to do so. For I declare that I have received no opinion of my conduct that has not been the most marked censure.'

resolute soldier—who, following the example of his father Haidar Ali, had endeavoured to compete with us for supremacy—lived there in considerable state and luxury, surrounded by the few faithful retainers who had survived the storm of Seringapatam. The bounty of the Company provided the means of enjoyment, and it was only in consonance with human nature if the memory of a former injury was embittered instead of being softened by the material benefits of the hour. But although the Muhammadan colony at Vellore was neither cordially disposed nor well behaved—for on several occasions murders and other acts of lawlessness committed by its members gave the Madras Government very serious anxiety and trouble—its opportunities of conspiring were too few to altogether justify the opinion that the disturbance was traceable to a systematic plot to restore the family of Haidar to the sovereign position in Mysore.

At the time of which we are speaking, the Sepoys of Madras still represented the élite of the native army. They were the representatives of the men who had fought under Eyre Coote and put an end to French pretensions at Wandiwash and Porto Novo. They were thought a great deal of by the Government, and the Company had regarded and treated them very much as pampered children. But at the beginning of the century new views were coming into force in military circles in India. What had seemed good enough to the old Company officers like

Lawrence and Munro, could not find toleration with English officers accustomed to the severer discipline and close attention to minute details in European armies. These changed views bore fruit in the issue of a number of regulations chiefly affecting the dress of the native soldier, and having as their main object the increased smartness of the Sepoy regiments on parade. In making these alterations there can be no doubt that too much consideration was paid to the pipe-clay traditions of European armies, and too little to the prejudices and sentiments of the native soldier.

On 14th November, 1805, an order was issued requiring the Sepoys to wear a new turban, the shape of which promised to ensure greater uniformity in the headgear of the Madras army. It was followed by a still more important and less reasonable change in a regulation published early in 1806, forbidding the Sepoys to wear their caste marks and earrings when in uniform. These alterations, authorised with a foolish absence of misgiving, were calculated to hurt the feelings of the Sepoys in their most susceptible part, in their religious and race distinctions as well as in social status, and to irritate them against the Government. The Commander-in-Chief of the Madras army, Sir John Cradock, afterwards Lord Howden, was mainly, if not solely, responsible for this interference.

The dissatisfaction of the Madras Sepoys was not long concealed. In April, 1806, the second battalion of the 4th regiment of Madras Native Infantry, one of the most distinguished regiments in the service, refused to wear the new turbans sent for their use. This open act of mutiny occurred at Vellore, where the battalion was quartered, and revealed the discontent which was prevalent throughout the whole of the Madras army. Although the ill-considered action of the authorities was the cause of the insubordination of a hitherto well-conducted and distinguished corps, it was impossible to overlook a flagrant defiance of orders by soldiers. In May, Sir John Cradock ordered a Court Martial to assemble for the trial of twenty-one Sepoys, who had acted as ringleaders, and in order to overawe the native troops a regiment of English cavalry—the 19th Dragoons—was sent to Vellore. The result of the trial was that the two principal offenders were sentenced to 900 lashes apiece, and then to be dismissed the army with ignominy, while the others were pardoned.

Neither the severity to those punished nor the clemency shown to those forgiven, however, allayed the irritation prevalent throughout the native army of Madras. In June, less than one month after the Court Martial, Sir John Cradock was beginning to entertain some apprehension about the scarcely-concealed discontent of the Sepoys, as to which he received alarming reports from more than one commanding officer. In considerable uncertainty, as well as anxiety of mind, he applied to the Governor of Madras to know what was best to be done, and his application is susceptible of the construction that he was willing to give way and sanction the withdrawal of the objectionable orders. Lord William Bentinck was in favour of a firmer attitude, stating that, whatever might have been the objection to passing the regulations in question, 'yielding in the face of force was to be avoided.' And thus by the decision of the Government of Madras the unpopular orders were upheld, and the discontent of the Sepoys became more intense.

On July 10th the native troops at Vellore threw off all the bonds of discipline and attacked their English officers and the small English force in garrison with them [1]. The attack was skilfully arranged. Not only were the Europeans surprised at the time when they were least prepared for attack, but the Sepoys cut them off from the arsenal and magazine. For many hours the nucleus of the English force held out against their more numerous assailants without ammunition. A summons was sent to the 19th Dragoons to proceed to Vellore in hot haste, and they arrived in time to relieve the besieged before the Sepoys could add to the massacre of the unarmed officers the overthrow of the small British force. Then a complete and effectual revenge was taken. The native regiments were scattered in all directions. Many hundreds of Sepoys were killed along the roads. The ringleaders who were not slain received their deserts from a Court

[1] The details of the fighting will be found in the History of the Madras Army by Lieut.-Colonel W. J. Wilson.

Martial less lenient than the one that had met a few months earlier. There was a fear for a time that the mutiny might extend from Vellore to Haidarábád; but all danger at the important station of Secunderábád was fortunately nipped in the bud by the energy and tact of Colonel Montresor. The objectionable orders as to dress, however, were cancelled by the express command of Lord William Bentinck, and the Vellore mutiny was at an end, except so far as it might serve as an historical warning of what happened fifty years later on a far larger and more terrible scale in Bengal.

A special Commission was duly appointed to critically examine and formally record all the circumstances that led up to this mutiny, and after a long examination of witnesses it assigned two causes for the mutiny, (1) the regulations as to dress, and (2) the residence of the Tipú family at Vellore. Sir John Cradock, who would naturally not be disposed to consider the former as the real cause, declared that in his opinion 'the turban grievance' was a mere pretext, and that the idea of re-establishing a Muhammadan dynasty was the main motive and object of the mutineers. On the other hand, Sir Thomas Munro, who knew Madras better than any other officer, gave his opinion, when asked by Lord William Bentinck, that 'the turban grievance' was the sole cause of the mutiny, and that there was a popular belief that it was the precursor of a scheme for the forcible conversion of the natives to Christianity. Sir Thomas

Munro held very strongly the opinion that it was not a Muhammadan plot at all, and scouted the idea of the Tipú family having any hand in it.

But the Honourable Court of Directors were not satisfied with the attitude of their representatives at Madras in face of one of the most unpleasant incidents in the whole experience of the Company. It was bad enough that the native soldiers, upon whom they principally relied to support their authority, should show signs of insubordination, but it was infinitely worse that that insubordination should be provoked by acts of their own executive, and that it should be successful in its object, for the obnoxious regulations were withdrawn. The opinion in Leadenhall Street was not merely that the Madras authorities had not shown themselves equal to the occasion, but that they did not realise the serious consequences that might have arisen from the mutiny at Vellore. That feeling inspired the most severe passages in the censure conveyed by the Court's letter of 15th April, 1807:—

'It seems to us that the Government, considered generally, did not exercise the discernment and vigilance which all the circumstances of the time required. With respect to Lord William Bentinck. Of the uprightness of his intentions and his regard for our service we have no doubt, and we have had pleasure in expressing our satisfaction with different measures of his government, but others, which we felt ourselves obliged in the course of the last year to disapprove, impaired our confidence in him, and after weighing all the considerations connected with the business of Vellore, we felt ourselves unable longer to continue that confidence to him which it is so necessary for a person holding his situation to possess.'

This despatch was tantamount to the recall of Lord William Bentinck from the Governorship of Madras, and it was accompanied by peremptory orders [1] for its immediate effect, which he felt very keenly as amounting, in his own words, to 'summary removal.' He ceased to be Governor of Fort St. George on 11th September, 1807. He complained bitterly of the want of consideration shown him, 'the orders of the Court being issued without waiting for the explanation of the officials accused,' and no arrangements being made for his passage to Europe, which he owed to the courtesy of the captain of a British man-of-war who happened to be on the Madras station. Before leaving Madras, Lord William Bentinck, with that regard for the welfare of his friends which never left him, entrusted their interests to Mr.

[1] The resolution passed by the Board of Directors reads as follows: 'Though the zeal and integrity of our present Governor of Madras, Lord William Bentinck, are deserving of our approbation, yet being of opinion that circumstances which have recently come under our consideration render it expedient for the interests of our service that a new arrangement of our Government of Fort St. George should take place without delay, we have felt ourselves under the necessity of determining that his Lordship should be removed, and we do hereby direct that Lord William Bentinck be removed accordingly.' Lord William Bentinck returned in the *Pitt*, Captain Bathurst, which vessel was only lent him after he had made a strong personal appeal, on family grounds, to the Admiral on the station, Sir Edward Pellew, afterwards Viscount Exmouth, the captor of Algiers.

William Petrie, senior member of Council, who succeeded him *ex officio* pending the arrival of his successor. On his return to Europe he sent his native secretary, Mútiah, a gold snuff-box in remembrance of their official connexion. The following extract from a letter from one of the highest civilians at Fort St. George, is of interest as showing what was thought at Madras at the time of the Court's action on the Vellore business:—

'As it affects the interests of my Honourable Masters under this Presidency I consider it a public misfortune, and as it respects your lordship individually I consider it an unjust and indecorous prejudication of a case not understood.'

After his return to England he presented in February, 1809, a memorial to the Court, of which the following is the most important passage:—

'The mutiny at Vellore cannot be attributed to me directly or indirectly, but I do assume to myself the merit, by a resolute adherence to a wise principle, an adherence in the face of obloquy and opposition, of having re-established order and confidence; of having thus averted the numerous calamities which the adoption of an opposite system of policy would have entailed on India, and ultimately on Great Britain; and above all of having saved the national character from disgrace. And what has been my recompense? I have been removed from my situation, and condemned as an accomplice in measures with which I had no further concern than to obviate their ill consequences. My dismissal was effected in a manner harsh and mortifying, and the forms which custom has prescribed to soften the severity of a misfortune at all events sufficiently severe were on this single occasion violated as if for the express purpose of deepening my disgrace. Whatever have been my errors, they surely have not merited a punishment than which a heavier could hardly have been awarded to the most wretched incapacity or the most criminal negligence. Under these circumstances I present myself to your notice. I take it for granted that the Court of Directors have been misinformed, and that to place the question before them in its true light is to obtain redress. My claims are not extravagant; I state them, and I trust moderately. I have been severely injured in my character and feelings; for these injuries I ask reparation; if, indeed, any reparation can atone for feelings so deeply aggrieved, and a character so unjustly compromised in the eyes of the world[1].'

Notwithstanding this appeal, the Court did not withdraw their censure or offer him the reparation which he claimed at their hands. Their reply stated that 'while again expressing their sense of his lordship's uprightness and zeal, and disclaiming any intention of personal disrespect, they still adhered to their original view, and regretted that greater care and caution had not been exercised in examining into

[1] In the year following the presentation of the memorial to the Court Lord William Bentinck published it, stating his reasons in the 'Advertisement.' 'I should think it unjust both to myself and my friends if I neglected to place within the reach of every inquirer the means of forming a correct judgment on the circumstances of that event. It will at least be satisfactory to me to know that if the subject should again excite discussion, either private or public, there will not be wanting an authentic testimony of the part which I acted on that occasion, of the principles by which I was guided, and of the manner in which my measures influenced the general course and result of affairs.'

the real sentiments and disposition of the Sepoys before measures of severity were adopted to enforce the order respecting the use of the new turban.' But although the Directors of the East India Company rejected Lord William Bentinck's appeal, and refused to grant him the amende he claimed at their hands in 1809, they atoned for this harshness eighteen years later, when they entrusted to his hands the charge, not of a single Presidency, but of the whole of India.

CHAPTER III

Military Service and Return to India

Before Lord William Bentinck's petition to the Court of Directors for reparation for his dismissal after the Vellore mutiny had been received and rejected, he had been entrusted with fresh active employment by the Government of his country, and was thus provided with the best cure for his injured feelings. While governing Madras he had attained in the natural course of promotion the rank of Major-General in the army, and when he reached England in 1808 he found that the preparations were far advanced for assuming a vigorous offensive in Portugal and Spain. During the earlier part of 1808 he commanded in Essex, but he solicited active employment, and in August of that year he was appointed to the staff of Sir Harry Burrard. Soon after the landing of the force commanded by that officer in Portugal he was sent by Sir Hew Dalrymple on a special mission to Madrid, to concert with the Spanish authorities the more vigorous plan of action rendered necessary by the imminent approach of Napoleon, who left Tilsit, after dividing the sovereignty of the world with

Russia, to assume in person the charge of the Spanish campaign. Lord William's efforts were only partially successful, as the Spanish commanders proved unequal to devising any hearty or effectual co-operation with us, and the rapid advance of the French on Madrid disarranged the plans that had been formed, and converted all ideas of an intended offensive into those of a strict defensive.

Under these circumstances the British Commissioners could do nothing better than quit the Spanish camp and hasten to join the English army with which Sir John Moore was advancing into Spain from Northern Portugal. Both the inadequacy of Spanish co-operation and the magnitude of the French plans rendered it prudent to convert that advance into a prompt retreat. Bentinck took an active part in the retreat to the coast, and at the battle of Corunna he commanded the brigade composed of the 42nd and 50th regiments, which bore the brunt of the fighting. He was honourably mentioned in the despatches of Sir John Hope, who succeeded to the command on the death of Moore. Having been promoted to the rank of Lieutenant-General, he served in the following year under Sir Arthur Wellesley in Portugal. His special knowledge of continental armies led to his being sent to Germany to raise a foreign legion, a task of no ordinary difficulty considering that Napoleon was then master of Central Europe, but which he succeeded in accomplishing. He was consequently under Wellington's orders for only a very short time, and when he finished his German commission he was entrusted with a separate and independent command of much responsibility.

The island of Sicily, which was given to Savoy by the Treaty of Utrecht and exchanged by that state for Sardinia with the Neapolitan Bourbons, had been one of the objects of Napoleon's ambition in the Mediterranean. Nelson had prevented the realisation of his plans so far as they were controlled by the sea, but the establishment of the kingdom of Naples under Joseph Bonaparte and his successor Murat compelled the Bourbons to take refuge in Sicily, which thus acquired increased importance from the desire of the French to acquire it and from our measures to thwart them. From the year 1806 to 1815 the independence of Sicily was only preserved by the presence of a considerable English garrison, and the officer in command of this force exercised a sort of discretionary control over all the acts of the Government of the island.

In 1811 Lord William Bentinck was appointed to the command of the English troops in Sicily. The internal affairs of the island, and the expectations formed as to a diversion from it into Eastern Spain exercising a favourable and decisive influence on the general war in the Peninsula, combined to make the post of special importance and to attract marked attention to its occupant. Lord William Bentinck was thus provided with an opportunity of much personal distinction, and of taking a considerable and definite part in the great struggle which was going on in every quarter of Europe. Perhaps it was his misfortune that his new post held out so many attractive opportunities of drawing European attention to his proceedings, and prevented his subordinating all his efforts to Wellington's main scheme in Spain. Had he devoted all his attention to co-operating in Eastern Spain with that commander there is no doubt that he would have placed his military reputation on a firmer basis, and that he would have contributed more largely than he did to the material ends of the war. Napier's estimate of his character here suggests itself, and may explain to the reader how it came about that he disobeyed instructions, and showed an inability to subordinate his will to the plans of others—'a man of resolution, capacity and spirit, just in his actions, and abhorring oppression, but of a sanguine impetuous disposition.'

The first year of Lord William Bentinck's residence in Sicily was employed in the organisation of the Sicilian army, which was raised to an effective strength of 10,000 men, while the English garrison amounted to half as many more. As the English fleet prevented all possibility of hostile attack, this considerable force was consigned to inaction at a period when it was essential to throw every available man into the field against the despot of the continent. The Italian troops made a good show on the parade ground, and great expectations were formed of their capacity to take a creditable part in the serious operations of war. When Lord William Bentinck arrived in Sicily the main task he had to accomplish was to organise as strong an Anglo-Italian expedition as he could, and to make a descent on the coast of Catalonia. There is no doubt that great results were anticipated from this diversion on the French flank, and the disappointment of the Duke of Wellington at the meagre outcome was in proportion to the hopes formed as to its consequences.

But before Lord William Bentinck could give his attention to military matters he had to compose a political difficulty of a pressing nature, and one with which his character and opinions[1] fitted him pre-eminently to deal. The Queen of Naples, who, under the influence of Lady Hamilton, had rendered such useful service to Nelson while France was still powerful on the sea, was neither the wisest nor the most forbearing of rulers when left to her own discretion. When that influence was withdrawn she seems to have imbibed an inveterate dislike of the English name and policy, and it has been stated that when she saw an Englishman she felt the guillotine at her neck. An explanation of this changed feeling has been attempted by alleging that after the marriage

[1] Blaquiere, an excellent authority, refers to the excitement in Sicily and the popular hope in the island on Lord William Bentinck's appointment. It is interesting to observe that when he first arrived in Sicily he formed certain definite opinions, and that he then hastened back to England in the *Cephalus* frigate to impress them upon the Government, and to obtain the necessary authority for his subsequent measures.

of Napoleon with the Arch-Duchess Marie Louise she wished to come to terms with him. But a more probable explanation is that she saw in English ascendency in Sicily an insuperable obstacle to the assertion of those privileges which alone rendered the possession of power of any value. For the Italian Bourbons, expelled from their mainland possessions, endeavoured to assert in Sicily, without regard to insular privileges, all the arbitrary power they had exercised at Naples.

This mode of proceeding gave rise to an amount of popular indignation that threatened to lead to disturbances, if not to civil war, and the first duty of the English commander was to terminate these domestic troubles and to reorganise the administration. Sicily required nothing less than a new constitution, and it was very much to the credit of Lord William Bentinck that he drew up one which gave general satisfaction, and which averted grave dynastic and popular trouble. The Queen of Naples was deposed; the King, whose incapacity was notorious, voluntarily resigned in favour of his son, and the Crown Prince was raised to the throne, while a House of Parliament was formed on the basis of our own. The Barons were recalled to Palermo, and the Queen was forbidden to enter that city, while Lord William Bentinck was declared Captain-General of all the troops. The new constitution was proclaimed amid popular applause to the Sicilian Parliament on July 20, 1812.

These internal affairs being settled, the projected

descent on Catalonia then came on for practical consideration. But on the eve of the departure of the Sicilian army Lord William Bentinck allowed his attention to be attracted to another object which promised in his eyes to achieve greater results and to exercise a more decisive influence on the European struggle than his active intervention in Spain. He received letters from the Russian Admiral, Tchighachoff, requesting his co-operation with a Russian army then quartered in Southern Russia, but with which he proposed to march across Bulgaria to the Adriatic, and thence crossing the sea to effect the liberation of Italy. It was Lord William Bentinck's favourite idea to promote the emancipation of Italy, and when this visionary scheme was submitted to him for support he yielded to the temptation, and dismissing the thoughts of Catalonia prepared to embark with all his resources on the new Italian adventure suggested by the Czar's representative. Not merely did he thus delay the arrival in Spain of the much-expected and sorely-needed reinforcements from Sicily, but by raising the sum of four million dollars at Gibraltar and Minorca for the benefit of the Russian expedition he depleted the most convenient money market, and added greatly to Wellington's difficulties at the most critical period of the Peninsular War. Wellington was naturally irritated by these occurrences, and he went so far as to call the Italian expedition Quixotic. The liberation of Italy, he said, was all very well, but the practical war after all was in Spain.

Nothing came of the proposed Russian descent on Italy. The Russian army did not carry out its march to the Adriatic, and Admiral Tchighachoff's plans faded into the air. Lord William Bentinck thus found himself at liberty in the autumn of 1812 to despatch to Catalonia the Anglo-Sicilian expedition which at an earlier date would, to say the least, have arrived more opportunely. Lord William Bentinck did not take personal command of the first expedition in 1812, which was not well managed, and effected little, although the French had the worst of the one engagement of any importance, at Alcoy. In the following year, however, he arrived from Sicily with a stronger force, increased by part of the garrison of Minorca. Sir Frederick Adam acted as second in command, and was placed at the head of the advance brigade. Marshal Suchet was detached from the main French army to hold the English expedition in check, and he carried out his instructions with skill and success. The English were successful in several minor affairs and advanced as far as the pass of Ordal. Here the French army opposed them in force, and after some fighting the English were obliged to retreat. Shortly after this repulse the Anglo-Italian expedition sailed back to Sicily *re infectâ*, and it cannot be said that Bentinck's military reputation was enhanced by this campaign. It may however be stated in fairness that Napier, in his criticism of this side-incident in the war, throws most of the blame on Sir Frederick Adam.

The return of the Anglo-Sicilian expedition to its starting-point was followed by the revival in a more practical form of the contemplated expedition into Italy. In March, 1814, when Napoleon's fortunes were shattered and he could with despairing courage alone defend the approaches to Paris, Lord William Bentinck, who had previously concluded a convention with Murat for his retention of the kingdom of Naples, landed at Leghorn at the head of 7000 men and called upon the Tuscans to effect the liberation of Italy. He marched rapidly along the coast viâ Spezia to Genoa, which the French garrison, although nearly as numerous as his own force, surrendered without any resistance. As a military achievement this campaign, in which Lord William Bentinck had the co-operation of an Austrian army under General (afterwards Prince) Nugent, was the most successful in which he was ever engaged. Yet even on this occasion his impulses led him to exceed his instructions.

His instructions were to observe a very discreet attitude towards the Italian people, whose aspirations towards liberty and unity were beginning to find expression, and to do nothing to fetter the hands of the allies in disposing of Genoa at the general peace. But his ardour outstripped his discretion and instructions. He was keenly alive to the injuries and aspirations of Italians, and he was one of the first English statesmen to believe that Italy could again be reawakened into a nation. Instead, therefore, of conforming to his instructions, which were dictated out of consideration for the natural expectations of Austria and the Bourbons, he called on the Tuscans to effect the liberation of Italy, and after the capture of Genoa he not only declared Italy free, but he restored the constitution which had formerly prevailed there. In his stirring address to the Genoese he said:—

> 'Warriors of Italy! only call and we will hasten to your relief, and then Italy by our united efforts shall become what she was in her most prosperous period and what Spain now is.'

It would take too long, and would be outside the purpose of this volume, to explain how it was that Lord William Bentinck was induced to believe that the moment was opportune for the revival of Italian independence, and that he might take a leading part in executing this scheme. But there is abundant evidence in his correspondence to show that the idea originated with the Sardinian minister, Alessandro Torri, and that it was encouraged by the Duke of Orleans, afterwards Louis Philippe, King of the French. The letters from that prince, who, having married the Princess Marie Amalie of Naples, found his most convenient residence at Palermo, reflect the highest credit on his political intelligence, and are marked by a personal regard for Lord William Bentinck that continued unabated to his death. But the advice they contained was incompatible with the realisation of the military plan, which would have thrown against the French in Spain all the British resources that were to be found in the Mediterranean.

One extract will illustrate the nature of this correspondence. In a letter dated 24th January, 1813, he advised Bentinck to 'withdraw his troops from Alicante to Mahon, as, whilst at Alicante, you are always exposed to see them pounced upon by the great Eagle of Ciudad Rodrigo' (Wellington).

The secret memorandum (20th January, 1812) with the Hereditary Prince Francis of Sicily, who, as described, was elevated to his father's position under the new constitution, stipulated that the object of a descent on Italy should be the freeing of the whole of Italy, and that the people should be left to select their own constitution. When these views became known at the Foreign Office they were not received with favour, but for a time Lord William Bentinck's explanation that they were necessary to procure the assistance of the people of Italy was accepted. When he wrote, 'hated as Murat is, the old dynasty is more so,' the words were not accepted literally. Lord William Bentinck was assumed to be carrying out his diplomatic mission at the court of the Neapolitan Bourbons, whereas he had been seized with a great idea, and was very much in earnest.

The more closely the events and relations of the contending parties in Italy at that time are considered the more diffident will any one be to say that Bentinck's project was chimerical. If England had made Italy, instead of Spain, the base of its operations against France, the influence we exercised on the continental struggle might have been still more decisive than it was, and from the Italian people we should have received far greater gratitude than we did from the inhabitants of the Iberian peninsula. But grand as was the idea of Italian unity in 1812, and feasible as the project might have become under the auspices of a great military genius like Wellington, we are constrained to admit that Lord William Bentinck was not such a commander, and that although as a statesman he realised what could be done, he did not possess as a soldier the qualities to carry out his noble project. He was the first English statesman to conceive the idea[1] of a modern kingdom of Italy, and to take some steps towards creating one. But he would have been more practical and better advised if he had subordinated his judgment to the Duke of Wellington and driven Suchet (as he could have done if he had employed all his resources) out of Catalonia in 1812. From a worldly point of view Louis Philippe was a bad adviser when he wrote entreating him to be careful not to let the Anglo-Sicilian forces 'be extracted from their peninsula for the benefit of the other one.'

[1] This was the more remarkable because he was on the most cordial terms with Austrian notabilities. Marshal Count Bellegarde, who commanded in 1813–4 in Lombardy, refers in his letters to their earlier intercourse in the most cordial terms. Count, afterwards Prince, Nugent was his most attached friend. The Archduke Francis D'Este of Austria, grandson of the Empress Maria Theresa, and, in right of his mother, representative of the last Duke of Este, confided all his plans to him, and when he recovered the State of Modena requested Bentinck's congratulations. His generous recognition of the merits of the Austrian army has been already quoted.

It must not be supposed that Lord William Bentinck's work in Italy was insignificant. After gaining possession of Genoa and restoring its independent constitution, he sent a small expedition to Corsica, and a General to act in his name and that of England to Milan. Both missions were crowned with complete success. The Corsicans expressed the wish to become British subjects, and the Milanese supported a proposition[1] to make the Duke of Cambridge King of Italy, with which scheme it was considered the Emperor of Russia was certain to be sympathetic. It will be seen from these facts that Lord William Bentinck's project was far from visionary, and that the idea of an united Italy was first put forward in a prominent and authoritative manner by Lord William Bentinck. It injured him materially with his Government. The idea of an independent Italy was incompatible with the restoration of the *status quo* effected at Vienna. He ceased to exercise the command over the British forces in the Mediterranean on 24th May, 1815, and when he presented himself at Naples in the following September he was refused permission to land; Lord Castlereagh acquiescing in this step on the ground that a dangerous use might have been made of his name. His sustained interest in Italy was shown by his taking up his residence at Florence, his studying the Italian language, and by his correspondence and intercourse with some of the most prominent public men of Italy.

[1] General Macfarlane's letter to Lord William Bentinck.

He resumed his connexion with English public life as member of Parliament for Lynn, but he seems to have devoted his attention mainly to the affairs of Italy and Sicily, where the constitution he had drawn up was set aside very soon after his departure and the expulsion of the French from Italy. In the year 1819 he was offered the Governorship of Fort St. George—his old post at Madras—but after consideration he refused this offer, because he considered that to send him back to the post he had been removed from twelve years before, under circumstances which he felt to be unjust, would be no adequate reparation of a wrong, and would show no proper appreciation of his own progress in political life and public reputation.

In 1822, when the return of the Marquis of Hastings from Bengal was announced, he made a representation of his claims to be nominated his successor, and he did not conceal from his friends that he would regard his selection as a gratifying vindication of his conduct in 1806. Lord Liverpool did not recognise the connexion between the two passages, and perhaps as the result of his proud declaration[1] that he took no steps to influence a vote, his claims were ignored in favour of Lord Amherst, who had led our second and abortive Embassy to the Court of China. It was this application that curiously enough brought him into connexion with James Mill, the historian. In Mrs. Grote's Life we are told that 'Mill thought him the

[1] His old friend Louis Philippe wrote of these events, 'You have shown yourself as frank and honourable as you have always been.'

best candidate, and so did every one else, but feared he had no chance.' The fear proved accurate, but although he was not destined to be Amherst's successful competitor, he was nominated his successor in 1827, and he was then brought into personal communication with Mill, to whom he made the curious confession, 'I must confess to you that what I have ever read amounts to very little, and that it is not without pain that I can read anything.' To Mill, perhaps on account of this confession, he appeared 'a well-intentioned but not a very well-instructed man.'

Lord Amherst's Governor-Generalship was marked by the Burmese war, which, on account of its expense, was unpopular with the Court of Directors, and it closed with a large deficit, which was a very unpleasant fact for the Company to face at a moment when it had to contemplate the reduction of its resources. The absolute necessity of economy and financial reform led it to think of the special care Lord William Bentinck had always shown in regulating finances, and to form the conclusion that a reforming and peaceful ruler might be a more useful representative under the prevailing circumstances than one of the type and temper of Wellesley and Hastings. Accordingly, in the summer of 1827 the Court selected Lord William Bentinck as its Governor-General in succession to Lord Amherst, thus healing the sense of injury in Lord William's mind in a satisfactory manner.

CHAPTER IV

FINANCIAL REFORMS AND SUPPRESSION OF CRIME

ALTHOUGH appointed to the Governor-Generalship in July[1], 1827, it was exactly twelve months later that Lord William Bentinck reached India. His predecessor, Lord Amherst, left India early in March, 1828, and in the interval the functions of the head of the administration were discharged by Mr. William Butterworth Bayley, then the chief representative of an Anglo-Indian family which has given many distinguished men to the public service. On July 4, 1828, the appointment of Lord William Bentinck as Governor-General, and of Viscount Combermere—the captor of Bhartpur — as Commander-in-Chief, was announced in Calcutta with the accustomed ceremony and salutes. The formal proceeding attached to the assumption of responsibility for the government of India was then of the simplest and least striking character. It consisted of a notice formally recorded among the minutes of Government that 'the Governor-

[1] In this same month died Sir Thomas Munro, Governor of Madras. Lord William Bentinck was in entire agreement with him on the subject of the ráyatwárí land-settlement, and Munro's opinion on the causes of the Vellore mutiny has already been quoted.

General acknowledged to have received an extract from a Public General Letter from the Court of Directors, dated April 5, 1793, and expressed his acquiescence thereto.' The proclamation of the new Governor-General was followed by the arrival of the customary letters of congratulation from the princes of India and the neighbouring states, among whom it may be stated that the King of Delhi, the Rájá of Nepál, and Ranjít Singh of the Punjab were prominent.

When Lord William Bentinck reached Calcutta, India was enjoying a brief interval of repose after many years of internal and external warfare. But the costly Burmese war had placed a severe strain on the financial resources of the country, and the most pressing matter of the day was to restore an equilibrium between the revenue and the expenditure. In 1828 the expenditure exceeded the receipts by more than a crore of rupees, or one million sterling. It was essential to remove this deficit, and economy was the first article in the programme of the new ruler, for, to use the words of Sir Charles Metcalfe, 'the Government which allows this to go on in time of peace deserves any punishment.' Although the Court of Directors had been very emphatic in their injunctions to Lord William Bentinck to economise and to restore the finances of India to a satisfactory footing, their instructions and suggestions as to how this was to be done were exceedingly vague except in one particular. On the subject of the reduction of Batta the Court gave the most positive and precise instructions, although the amount to be saved was trifling and the umbrage given to a large body of their servants excessive. The Batta difficulty was the first with which Lord William Bentinck had to deal in India, and the personal odium he incurred from faithfully carrying out the orders of his employers does not seem to have wholly left him during the seven years he served in that country.

Batta, or more correctly Bhát'ha, is a Hindi and Maráthá word meaning 'extra or additional pay.' The Company, very soon after it commenced what may be termed its political career, had granted batta to its military officers. The amount varied with the services rendered and the place at which the officer happened to be stationed. Thus full batta was given for active service within the Company's territories. It was doubled during any expedition or service beyond the frontier. When, however, the officer was stationed during peace at any place where quarters were provided for him, he only received half batta. Long usage had made the officer regard this addition to his pay as his inherent right, and many of the highest authorities on the subject had declared that the Company's officers, especially those of junior rank, could not possibly subsist on their ordinary pay if this allowance were reduced or withdrawn. Both the Marquis of Hastings and Lord Amherst had addressed remonstrances to the Court of Directors when they were directed to reduce the batta allowance, and their influence had been sufficient to postpone the change.

At length the Court of Directors would listen to no further objections, and Lord William Bentinck was peremptorily ordered to carry out the reduction of batta to one-half its fixed amount. He was left no option in the matter, and he could only obey the orders which accompanied his appointment. As Sir Charles Metcalfe truly said, 'the order was one which could not have been disobeyed unless we could tell the Court that we are supreme and they subordinate.' In November, 1828, an order was issued reducing the batta allowance to one-half at Dinápur, Barrackpur, Berhampur, Dum Dum, and eventually at Gházípur, which were the five principal stations of the Bengal army. It may be easy to imagine, but it is certainly difficult to describe, the commotion caused by this order among the officers of the Company's service. Indignant remonstrances were presented by all the officers affected by the change, couched in language that showed none of the restraint imposed by discipline, and accusing the Government of breach of faith. The Commander-in-Chief himself drew up a remonstrance, and these documents were forwarded to London by Lord William Bentinck, who stated in reply to the memorialists that 'it would afford him sincere gratification if the Court should see fit to reconsider their orders.'

But the Court of Directors were prepared for and unmoved by the clamour of their military officers.

The tone of the remonstrances was declared to be unbecoming, and they asserted their right to reduce or to increase the pay of all persons in their employ. In their final reply of March, 1830, they declared that the reduction must be carried out, and that it had the sanction of the Duke of Wellington and the other members of the Government at home. This order was published in India in September of the same year, and definitely settled the question, although it could not allay the irritation of which Lord William Bentinck became the principal mark and victim. The saving effected by this reduction was about £20,000 a year, but it seems possible that the Court at one time thought of abolishing batta altogether, and that the opposition and agitation its first orders excited may not have been barren of result in preventing the execution of a more sweeping measure. In one respect the batta question threw light on Lord William Bentinck's character. During the whole of the controversy from 1828 to 1830 the Calcutta Press teemed with personal attacks on him, often of an abusive nature, but he never thought of using the large repressive measures in his power. It was at this time that he said 'he knew of no subject which the Press might not freely discuss.' When, however, the final orders of the Court were to be published, he decided that the season of discussion had passed away, and for the first and only time[1] in his Indian career he issued

[1] This apparent inconsistency in his Press policy is fully explained by Sir John Kaye in his Life of Lord Metcalfe, pp. 253-4.

a minute (September 6, 1830) forbidding the Press to comment upon the Court's decree on the subject of batta.

More important economies remained to be effected than the clipping of military pay, and by reductions in the administration of the land revenue, the Provincial Courts, and the costly settlements in the Straits of Malacca, he proceeded to carry out the principal portion of the mission with which he had been charged, and to restore an equilibrium to the finances. But these measures of detail would have failed to produce a result commensurate with the expectations and necessities of the Company, if there had not been executed at the same time a great reform of principle in the systematic employment of natives of India in administrative offices which had hitherto been reserved exclusively for Englishmen. This important change, which will come under consideration more appropriately at a later stage of Lord William Bentinck's Indian career, was rendered imperative by the cost of a purely English administration and by the inability of the Indian revenue to meet it. Economy in establishment and efficiency in revenue-collection might have provided a palliative for the evil which arose from the incontestable fact that the conquests of the Company after Clive, however inevitable, were for a time unprofitable from a revenue standpoint. There was no real cure save that applied by Lord William Bentinck, and adopted by the Government and people of England as a cardinal point in their Indian policy.

Among the measures taken to effect economy may

be mentioned the appointment of two committees, one military and one civil, to investigate the whole expenditure and to report wherever reductions could be made. At the same time large reductions were ordered in the military establishments of the three Presidencies. The Provincial Courts of Appeal and Circuit, which had become proverbial for their dilatoriness and uncertainty of decision, were abolished, to the promotion of justice and economy at the same time. While the recommendations of the committee entrusted with the supervision of the civil establishment resulted in the eventual saving, after some years, of an annual sum of half a million sterling, the orders of the Court for the reduction of its military forces retrenched more speedily the sum of one million for the Exchequer. The Government very rightly looked to an increase of receipts as well as to a decrease of expenses for providing the way out of its difficulties. The settlement of the land revenue in the North-West Provinces, effected by Mr. Robert Merttins Bird, produced beneficial results, which were not diminished by the establishment of a separate Board of Revenue at Allahábád. This measure, from which the greatest benefits ensued, and of which it was said that it 'was completed upon principles equally conducive to the improving resources of the state and the growing prosperity and happiness of the people,' was not finally carried into effect until the year 1833. It proved itself to be a comprehensive and successful scheme for raising an increased revenue from the soil of a large division of India.

In another direction Lord William Bentinck took important steps of enduring consequence for increasing the revenue from the much-reviled but indispensable item of opium. Over the Bengal produce the East India Company possessed complete control, and as long as Central India was distracted by war the competition of the opium-producing districts in that part of the country was not to be feared. But the close of the Maráthá wars had led to a large increase in the production of Málwá opium, and unless Bengal opium was to be undersold by that exported from Indian ports not subject to the Company, it was essential for the Government to obtain some share in the profit of that trade and some control over its expansion. The favourite route for the export of Málwá opium was through Rájputána to Karáchi, whence it was sent viâ Diu and Damán in ships flying Portuguese colours to China. It was quite clear that as this opium was sold at a much lower price than that from Patná, the revenue of the Company would be adversely affected unless some measures could be taken to divert the export of Málwá opium to Bombay.

Several tentative measures had been tried, only however to result in failure, before Lord William Bentinck carried out a plan for licensing the direct conveyance of opium from Málwá to Bombay, thus avoiding the circuitous route to Karáchi, and ensuring to the Company some share in the profit. After numerous attempts to coerce the princes and to deprive the people of their legitimate rights because they encroached on a treasured preserve of the Company, this arrangement put an end to the difficulty, and placed the matter on the satisfactory basis on which it still exists. Like the settlement of the land revenue in the North-West, it deserves all the credit due to a skilful and successful piece of practical administration. In close connexion with this opium arrangement, and in some degree emanating from it, was the institution of an inquiry into the question of internal transit duties, which, after Bentinck left India, resulted in the abolition of those fetters on the commercial development of the country. The economies described, and the increased revenue raised, resulted, before the departure of Lord William Bentinck, in converting what had been a deficit of one million into a surplus of two millions.

The measures taken to effect administrative reforms and to introduce native agency into the dispensation of justice claim passing notice, although it is right to state that the proposals upon which the Government eventually took action were made and approved before Lord William Bentinck arrived in India. The Provincial Courts, saddled with an excess of duties, had proved unable to get through the work entrusted to them. Arrears accumulated, accused persons, whether innocent or not, were detained in prison for an unnecessary period, and the assessment of land could only be fixed after long and tedious delays. With a view to remedying this state of things, magistrates and collectors were placed under the supervision of Commissioners of Revenue and Circuit, who were to make frequent tours within their jurisdiction, and to be in constant touch with the people. Experience showed the wisdom of depriving them of some of their judicial functions, and this led to the increasing importance of the judges in the country, of whom, by a change in the system of appointment, many were to be natives. Lord Cornwallis in his settlement of Bengal had given to Europeans, with insignificant exceptions, the control over the civil and criminal jurisdiction, but it soon became evident that a sufficient staff could not be maintained to deal efficiently with the work to be done. Hence the deadlock arose that has been described. The only remedy for the evil was the employment of natives, and after some years' delay in taking what was the very natural course of trying ordinary native offenders by a native tribunal, native magistrates were nominated and permitted to deal with the majority of those who broke the law. In 1827 'nearly nineteen-twentieths of the original suits instituted in the civil courts throughout the country were already determined by native judicial officers.' On the eve also of Lord William Bentinck's arrival in India a new and higher grade of native judges, with the style of Sadr Amins, was created, qualified to hear appeals from the ordinary Amins. This step was followed up by the establishment of a Court of Sadr Diwání and Nizámat Adálat at Allahábád, with authority to hear appeals that before its creation would have had to be sent to Calcutta. Although not primarily responsible for these measures, Lord William Bentinck cordially approved of them, and supported every project to give increased dignity and confidence to the native judges. In this manner was the co-operation of the natives of India secured in the department of government wherein it would produce the most advantageous consequences, and be attended with the fewest drawbacks. The employment of natives of India in trying their fellow-countrymen, with whose ways and feelings they were thoroughly familiar, was open to no possible objection, and conduced at the same time to both economy and despatch in the disposal of business.

It will be appropriate at this stage to refer to the intimate relations which subsisted between Lord William Bentinck and Sir Charles (afterwards Lord) Metcalfe, a man who took a prominent part in the reforms described and those to follow, and who carried out several of the schemes left over for final execution when Lord William Bentinck quitted India in 1835. In the great work of entrusting larger executive and judicial powers to the natives Sir Charles Metcalfe might claim as prominent a place as his chief, and it was he who first defined in the following passages the best organisation for the joint European and Native administration of India:—

'The best form of government with a view to the welfare of the natives of India in their present state I believe to be that which is most simple and most free from artificial institutions. The best form of government with a view to the maintenance of British dominion in India I believe to be that which is most conducive to a union of powers and most free from the elements of collision and counteraction.'

His plan of government was—

'Native functionaries in the first instance in all departments. European superintendents, uniting the local powers of judicature, police and revenue, in all their branches through the districts over which they preside. Commissioners over them, and a Board over the Commissioners communicating with and subject to the immediate control of the Government.'

The relations of these two men with each other did not at first promise to attain the cordiality that they eventually acquired. The entries in his diary show that Sir Charles Metcalfe was favourably impressed with the new ruler of India from the first, but they also bear testimony to the fact that to all appearance Lord William Bentinck did not reciprocate the feeling. Three weeks after the Governor-General reached Calcutta Metcalfe wrote, 'I like the little that I have seen of our new Governor-General very much—he is a straightforward, honest, upright, benevolent, sensible man;' and again he wrote a few days later, he is 'a very benevolent, unaffected, open, candid, kind man whom every one I conceive must like.' But while thus cordially recognising his merits he also notes, with a tone of regret, the absence of all response. 'He and I do not approximate, which is rather surprising to me, for many of our sentiments are in common with both of us.' The removal of this coolness was due, strangely enough, to the stimulating effect of a despatch from Lord Ellenborough, the President of the Board of Control, on the subject of our policy in India, which certainly entitles that often-abused Governor-General to some share in the credit of the reformed administration with which the name of Lord William Bentinck is specially associated. In that despatch it is stated that—

'We have a great moral duty to perform to the people of India. We must, if possible, give them a good and permanent government. In doing this we confer a greater benefit upon the people of this country than in sacrificing the interests of India to the apparent present interests of England. The real interests of both countries are the same. The convulsion which would dissolve their connexion would entail much loss on us and bring desolation upon India.'

On receiving this despatch Lord William Bentinck at once wrote to Sir Charles Metcalfe in the following terms, and thus began that personal friendship and close political co-operation which continued during the remainder of their public careers:—

'Anxious as I must be to answer to this call, but sensible at the same time of my own incompetency to the task, I can only obtain the information Lord Ellenborough wants by a recourse to greater experience and knowledge. In this difficulty I confidently apply to you for that assistance which no man in India is better able to afford.'

From that time forward Sir Charles Metcalfe, who succeeded Mr. Butterworth Bayley in November, 1829, as Deputy-Governor and Vice-President of the Council—the highest office in the service after the Governor-Generalship—was closely associated with Lord William Bentinck in all the acts of administration. His advice was on every occasion respectfully sought, and when Lord William Bentinck laid down in 1835 the functions of supreme authority, he accorded to this colleague a most generous recognition. At the Calcutta dinner on the eve of his departure he said that he had 'never met with the individual whose integrity, liberality of sentiment, and delicacy of mind excited in a greater degree his respect and admiration.'

One of the first and not the least important administrative measures carried out by Lord William Bentinck was the strenuous and systematic effort to suppress the Thags in their practice of murder for the purposes of robbery. The complete success which crowned the steps taken for this purpose in the first year of his administration, and which were maintained with equal energy and vigilance during its whole course, render the suppression of *thagí* one of the most notable achievements of the Governor-Generalship of Lord William Bentinck.

The story of the proceedings taken against the Thags is told in the fullest official detail in five volumes of manuscript records preserved in the India Office. Therein will be found not merely particulars of the capture of the different gangs, exact reports of the trials and sentences, and precise returns of the expenditure entailed, but also genealogical tables of the principal Thags, showing that their nefarious trade had become a family profession and secret.

Thag is the Hindustani for 'cheat,' and the name strictly translated gives no indication of their mode of perpetrating the dreadful crime that rendered them the terror of the Indian traveller. The less usual but more correct name of phánsi-gár gives a clearer insight into their practices, for phánsa means noose, the fatal rope or scarf with which they strangled their unsuspecting and defenceless victims. The phánsa plays a prominent part in the Hindu mythology and is assigned to several gods and goddesses as their favourite weapon. The exact date at which highway robbers adopted it for the purposes of their vocation is uncertain or unknown, but the French traveller Tavernier, in the middle of the seventeenth century, mentions the stranglers of the highway as one of the dangers of travel in the dominions of the Great Mogul. The troubles of the eighteenth century, when the destinies of India hung at the mercy of military adventurers and lawless hordes of plunderers, added undoubtedly to their numbers, and the whole of Central India from Haidarábád to Oudh, and Bundelkhand to Rájputána, provided a vast and profitable field for the display of their skill as secret murderers.

Their mode of proceeding may be thus briefly described. Having performed certain propitiatory rites of a quasi-religious character, and obtained some favourable prognostications as to the result of their enterprise—for the fatalism which characterised their religious belief and gave fortitude to their proceedings was largely tinged with superstition—they set out along one of the main roads frequented by merchants and other travellers. To all appearance they were a party of unarmed and harmless men, either pursuing their business as traders or returning to their native village from a pilgrimage. In those days of open highway robbery travellers were only too glad to meet with companions, and the Thags never experienced any difficulty in picking up one, or more than one, unsuspecting wayfarer *en route*. There was nothing in their demeanour or conduct to excite suspicion. At the well or the caravanserai they seemed like the most inoffensive of travellers, and the only ground for suspicion was that which least arouses it, a special cheerfulness of manner and a conciliatory attitude towards all strangers. Having once selected the victim their patience in waiting for the most favourable moment to strike the blow was remarkable, and constituted the main secret of their power and protracted impunity. Sometimes they would deem it expedient to strike at once, but more often they would perform a journey of days and weeks together with their intended victim before they would deliver the fatal blow. But in nearly all cases it was done at a moment when the victim would be least prepared and most off his guard—either engaged in his prayers or at ablutions—and the noose was always used with such deadly precision that the murdered person never had a chance of raising an alarm. The larger proportion of victims were single individuals, but if the gang was sufficiently numerous, and sometimes the Thags travelled in bands of sixty or seventy, they would not be afraid to entice a considerable body of travellers and to murder as many as a dozen at a single massacre. In all cases they resorted to every precaution to prevent surprise from interruption, and with such success that no instance of failure is recorded.

The younger members of the family or band served their apprenticeship as scouts, and it was only after many years of experience in this innocent capacity that they were allowed to so much as witness the perpetration of the crime, while the act of throwing the scarf was always entrusted to the most expert and experienced Thag. Their skill in effecting the murder of their victims was matched by the secrecy with which they disposed of their remains, and sometimes the most conclusive evidence against a captured Thag was the discovery of the skeletons of the murdered in an unlikely spot, revealed by the confession of a confederate. The strictness of the discipline was softened by the ties of family, and the secrets of the brotherhood were preserved by the invocation of religion as much as by the terror of the severe punishment meted out to treachery.

The disturbed condition of India during the whole of the eighteenth century added largely, as has been said, to the number of the Thags, whose reputation was greatly enhanced in the popular mind by the practical impunity with which their operations were carried on. If their own account of themselves might be accepted, they originally formed a special colony divided into seven tribes and located near Delhi. In those days they were said to be all Muhammadans, but the beliefs and regulations of the caste were essentially Hindu of a corrupt kind, and when the Thags were brought before British Courts of Justice the majority were found to be of Hindu race. It is probable from this statement that they were at first a local pest in the neighbourhood of the Mughal capital, where their enormities soon attracted notice. The Muhammadan Emperors were strong enough to banish the offenders to a distance from their capital, but not to break up their organisation. They left Delhi, and scattering themselves throughout Central India and the Deccan found a more profitable arena for their exploits.

They were commencing the career of extended mischief which made them known throughout India when the French traveller, Tavernier, noted their depredations as one of the gravest perils to the traveller in the peninsula. They flourished during the whole of the eighteenth century on the troubles of India, and in the absence of any central power or authority to call them to account. The officials of many of the smaller states, finding themselves unable to cope with the malefactors, made common cause with them, and for a share in the profits accorded them the protection that was provided by their own inertness and indifference. Their numbers and their success steadily increased, until at the end of the last century they were brought into contact with our power. The annexations of Mysore and Chitor were followed by the dispersion of some of the most formidable bands, and the majority of the survivors withdrew into the native states of Málwá and Rájputána, where for another thirty years they enjoyed security and immunity from official pursuit. In the time of both Lord Hastings and Lord Amherst several bands were discovered and broken up, but such was the feeling of toleration or fear with which they were regarded by the native courts and officials, that the conviction of the prisoners was by no means the certain consequence of their capture, and it is correct to say that when Lord William Bentinck took up the matter nothing had been done to break up the Thags as an organisation hostile to the community.

In 1829 special orders and fuller powers were given to Mr. F. C. Smith, Agent to the Governor-General in the Narbadá Territories—a division corresponding to the present Central India Agency and Central Provinces combined—to proceed against all Thags, and to put down their associations with the strong hand. Major Sleeman, whose name will always be honourably coupled with the disappearance of this crime in India, was given a special appointment as his coadjutor and assistant. Other officers were at a later period entrusted with a similar task, when it was found by practical experience that the Thags embraced too wide an area to be dealt with by a single officer or a local department, and among them it is only just that the names of Major (afterwards Sir John) Low in Oudh, of Mr. Wilson in Bundelkhand, and of Colonel Stewart in Haidarábád, should be mentioned as among the most energetic and successful.

The active operations of the Thag department covered a period of six years, and during that time two thousand Thags were arrested. Of these fifteen hundred were sentenced either to death or to different periods of transportation. Although there had been no attempt on the part of the native governments to proceed against the malefactors, it was gratifying to find that once the British Government took up the matter the darbárs of the principal States, such as Haidarábád, Oudh, and Gwalior, hastened to lend their hearty and useful co-operation. This was the more satisfactory and necessary, inasmuch as the headquarters of some of the largest gangs were to be found within the Native States. The readiness of the Native Governments to associate themselves with us in a work that was not merely beneficial to the community, but which might be termed essential from the point of view of humanity, was not, however, imitated by the Native Courts, where the judges showed a tendency to deal too lightly with captured Thags, and availing themselves of any deficiency in the evidence as to murder to evade the infliction of capital sentences. The possibility of administrative energy being neutralised by judicial timidity was averted by plenary judicial powers being conferred on Mr. Smith, and the sentences passed on convicted Thags were thenceforward in just proportion to the enormity of the crime.

The final result of these sustained and systematic efforts to suppress the crime was that all the principal bands were broken up, that the reputation of the Thags was destroyed, and that the most formidable murder association which India had ever known passed out of existence. More than fifty years have elapsed since the labours of the Commission presided over by Mr. Smith and Major Sleeman were brought to an end, and, although there have been isolated cases, there has been no attempt to revive the old organisation.

The family secrets and ties which constituted the strength of the fraternity have died out or been dissolved by the lapse of time, and it may be doubted whether the crime in its old form could be revived, even were India to pass through another of those troubled periods which formed so large a part of her history, and from which she seems now happily to be rescued. Strictly speaking, the suppression of the Thags was due to the active and energetic measures of the Indian administration rather than to the policy of Lord William Bentinck, but he vigorously supported the measures taken against them, and urged on his lieutenants to make a speedy end of these enemies of the public peace. It must also be noted to his credit that when he took up the reins of office the Thags were more formidable than they had ever been before, and that when he left India they were shattered and practically annihilated.

CHAPTER V

THE ABOLITION OF WIDOW-BURNING

A MEMORABLE act of Lord William Bentinck's government, and the one with which his name will be most prominently associated in history, was the abolition of Widow-burning. It is permissible to think that the educational and administrative reforms which he introduced were of more permanent importance and exercised a wider influence upon our position in India; but the abolition by a short resolution of a practice sanctioned by religion and the usage of centuries was more calculated to arrest public attention and to obtain general applause than measures passed from time to time at the Council-board, of which the full effect could only become apparent after the lapse of years. The abolition of *satí* resembled the suppression of *thagí* in this respect, that it was also an act of humanity; but whereas the community generally regarded the Thags as murderers and robbers, those who performed the *satí* were held up as model wives, and as paragons of virtue. With the full acquiescence of the people the

Thags were destroyed, but it was in opposition to the people and with the support of very few Hindu reformers that *satí* was abolished through our overwhelming sense of an obligation to humanity. Of that sentiment Lord William Bentinck made himself the exponent and executor.

The practice of *satí*[1] from our first appearance on the Ganges, the part of India in which it was most in vogue, had attracted the attention and roused the disapprobation of our officers. Repugnant as the act of self-immolation was to our ideas, it was rendered worse by the knowledge that the sacrifice was in many cases not voluntary, and that the victim was only rendered capable of playing her part by the use of drugs. But in those days there was a wide gulf between disapprobation and active legislative repression. It was the firmest article in the faith of the East India Company that all the customs of the natives should be scrupulously respected, and that nothing should be done to give umbrage to their religious prejudices. The policy thus defined was unquestionably the wisest and the best, and it has been consistently adhered to during the whole of our rule in India. The only departures made from it have been taken under some paramount sense that an

[1] 'The term suttee or satí is strictly applicable to the person, not the rite; meaning "a pure and virtuous woman," and designates the wife who completes a life of uninterrupted conjugal devotedness by the act of Saha-gamana, accompanying her husband's corpse. It has come in common usage to denote the act.' Wilson, British India, vol. ix. p. 185.

outrage not sanctioned by God, and disapproved of by the higher conscience of the Indians themselves, was being perpetrated, shocking to the human mind, and amounting to a scandal on our administration. Such a departure has to be recorded in the measures taken against *satí* by Lord William Bentinck, for reasons given in the masterly minute which concludes this chapter, and which has never before been printed.

The practice of *satí* had been in force for so many centuries that it was an archaic and useless question for the English administrator to inquire whether it was really in accordance or not with the injunctions of the early Hindu religion. As we always abstained from playing the part of religious instructors to the people, it mattered little to us whether Widow-burning was part of the original faith of the Hindus, or an innovation and abuse grafted on it by male legislators in a society which ranked female life at a low value, and thought only of enhancing the pride and dignity of the husband. The practice had the sanction of antiquity and the approbation of the Hindu people. It formed an essential feature in their daily religious life, and it would have been absurd for us to interfere with it on the ground that we knew the Hindu religion better than its own priests and followers. Such an argument might be urged by native reformers, like Dwarakanath Tagore and Rammohun Roy, who, moved by their spirit of humanity to detestation of a senseless and brutal sacrifice, strove to convince their countrymen that *satí* was not enjoined by the code of Manu, and that it was even opposed to the gentle and benign nature of their original faith.

Our intervention could only be based on the ground of administrative necessity, and on the duty to put down what Hindus might call a sacrifice, but what the rest of the civilised world was agreed in denouncing as a crime. The presence of the native reformers named, and the expression, however slow and slight, of what might be called a more educated and higher native opinion under their auspices, supplied an argument in favour of the abolition of *satí* by suggesting that after all native opinion was not unanimous on the subject, and that the sentiment of the most enlightened Hindus vindicated in anticipation the action of the British Government. But there can be no doubt that even if there had been no native reformers, and no intelligent native opinion, the action of the British Government would not have been deferred. The knell of *satí* had struck when Lord William Bentinck reached India.

Expediency and the reluctance to increase the difficulties with which we had always to cope, by stirring up any popular fermentation, caused the postponement of decisive action, but from our earliest appearance in Bengal, our disapprobation of the rite was unqualified. In the time of the Marquis Cornwallis, British officers, although prohibited from preventing the rite, were specially ordered on all occasions to withhold their consent to its performance whenever their acquiescence might be invited. They were to show by their attitude that although the British Government did not interfere to stop the sacrifice, they regarded it with emphatic and unequivocal disapproval. The Marquis Wellesley, notwithstanding the disturbed and hostile condition of India in his time, wished to take steps for its summary suppression without passing any measure of the legislature, but simply by treating every participator as an ordinary offender. With this view he submitted the question to the Nizámat Adálat, but the judges did not fall in with his views, more however on the ground of expediency than of abstract right. Their view was that the abolition of *satí* might be effected gradually and within a reasonable period, and they made certain suggestions with this object. While respecting the rite as a religious observance, they proposed several enactments calculated to remove the abuses which had grown up around the original office. They would, for instance, have made it a penal offence to drug an intending *satí*, or to take any part in forcing an unwilling woman to the funeral pyre, and they no doubt anticipated the custom dying a natural death from the absence of voluntary self-immolators. But their suggestions were not incorporated in any legislative measure, and encouraged by the inertness of the British Government, or by its inability to devise a remedy, the practice increased rather than diminished in the valley of the Ganges.

But the increased prevalence of the practice stirred

the executive into action, and one of the last steps taken by Lord Minto before his departure in 1813 was to incorporate the suggestions made by the Nizámat Adálat eight years before into the form of circular instructions to all the judicial authorities. These ordered the British officials to abandon their former attitude of indifference and rigid abstention from interference. Instead of withholding their consent, their consent was made essential to the performance of the rite. Information of an intended *satí* had to be given to the nearest magistrate, or failing a magistrate, police officer, and it was their first duty to ascertain whether the widow went to her fate of her own free will, or under any form of compulsion. Other precautions were taken to ensure that the act should be one rather of folly than brutality. No widow was to be immolated who was less than sixteen or who happened to be pregnant; the use of drugs was strictly prohibited; and the police were always to be present at the sacrifice, not merely to ensure order, but also to afford the victim the opportunity up to the very last of changing her mind and saving her life.

However well intentioned these instructions were, they proved in fact quite inadequate to attain their end. The practice of *satí* continued with unabated vigour, and the attendant abuses, far from disappearing, were as rife as before they were issued. The police were often sympathetic to the promoters of the sacrifice, and native ingenuity easily baffled official inquiry as to age, condition, and the use of intoxicants. The number of *satís* steadily increased after this change of policy, and the number of widows immolated in a single year in the Lower Provinces alone sometimes exceeded 800, while the average for the ten years prior to 1828 did not fall below 600. According to some authorities the stipulation that the consent of the British representative was essential to the performance of the sacrifice strengthened the hold that the practice had acquired on the Hindu mind, for the report was spread by the priests and easily accepted by the populace that the Government had made itself a party to the ceremony. According to others the increased number of *satís* was only a matter of more accurate returns owing to the police supervision, or perhaps the result of a greater mortality during the years named. However that may be, the interference (partial and one-sided as it may be termed) of the executive brought to light the fact that the practice of *satí* was as extensive as report alleged, and that many hundreds of innocent lives were sacrificed brutally and without cause every year. That the attention of the Government was directed to these facts, and that the need of repressive measures was becoming evident at Calcutta before Lord William Bentinck arrived in India, is clearly shown by the important expression of opinion from the Marquis of Hastings quoted in the Minute already referred to. The Marquis of Hastings wrote in reply to Lord William Bentinck's enquiry:—

'The subject which you wish to discuss is one which must interest one's feelings most deeply, but it is also one of extreme nicety when I mention that in one of the years during my administration of government in India above 800 widows sacrificed themselves within the Provinces comprised in the Presidency of Bengal, to which number I very much suspect that very many not notified to the magistrates should be added. I will hope to have credit for being acutely sensible to such an outrage against humanity. At the same time I was aware how much danger might attend the endeavouring to suppress forcibly a practice so rooted in the religious belief of the natives. No men of low caste are admitted into the ranks of the Bengal army. Therefore the whole of that formidable body must be regarded as blindly partial to a custom which they consider equally referrible to family honour and to points of faith. To attempt the extinction of the horrid superstition without being supported in the procedure by a real concurrence on the part of the army would be distinctly perilous. I have no scruple to say that I did believe I could have carried with me the assent of the army towards such an object. That persuasion, however, arose from circumstances which gave me peculiar influence over the Native Troops.'

Lord Hastings expressed in this letter very clearly the prevalent dread that the most serious objection to the suppression of *satí* was the disturbing effect it might produce on the discipline and allegiance of the Bengal native army, at the same time that he affirmed his own belief that he personally could have influenced the sepoy so far as to induce him to remain passive while he carried out this great reform. His successor, Lord Amherst, shared the same opinion, while he had no similar confidence in his hold upon the affection of the native troops; and his views were summed up in the following passage, taken from a letter to the Court:—

'Nothing but apprehension of evils infinitely greater than those arising from the existence of the practice should induce us to tolerate it for a single day.'

Before Lord William Bentinck arrived in India there had therefore been from the highest British authorities in that country several expressions of opinion that the practice of *satí* was an act of inhumanity, and that it ought to be abolished. At the same time they confessed that the danger of arousing native distrust and hostility by an act interfering with this religious custom was exceedingly great, and they shrank from making the experiment. They would not have hesitated to face the opposition if it were not coupled, as they feared it would be, with the insubordination of the native army. The effect it would be likely to produce on the Bengal troops was the chief deterrent to passing a necessary reform in the minds of Lord William Bentinck's predecessors, who were as sensible as he was of the inhumanity of *satí*.

Such was the position of the question when Lord William Bentinck assumed the reins of office. The weight of experience was against stirring up unnecessary agitation and danger by grappling with it. The instructions of the Court of Directors, if they did not fetter the action of their delegate, at least inculcated the need of caution. The personal experience of Lord William Bentinck, as he somewhat bitterly reminds the reader of his minute in connexion with the Vellore mutiny, was opposed to any hazardous legislation. There was no incumbent duty for him to deal with the question at all. He might have passed it on to his successor in the same manner as his predecessors had passed it on to him. He might have accepted the dictum of the Marquis of Hastings that it required great personal influence with and a certain ascendency over the native troops to carry such a measure successfully, and he could have truthfully declared that he did not possess the influence of the conqueror of the Maráthás and the pacificator of Central India. Or he might have based his refusal to act in the matter on Lord Amherst's not unreasonable 'apprehension of evils infinitely greater than those arising from the existence of the practice.' But he at once, and without hesitation, came to the conclusion that he could not remain indifferent to this crime and abstain from action against it without himself being guilty of 'the crime of multiplied murder.'

The vague apprehension of popular discontent and opposition resolved itself, as has been said, into the very definite and precise fear that the Bengal army would revolt as the direct consequence of any measure passed for the abolition of *satí*. The essential preliminary to any safe legislation was to ascertain the true feelings of that army, and it was in this direction that Lord William Bentinck first took action by addressing a confidential letter to 'forty-nine officers pointed out to me by the Secretary to Government in the Military Department, as being from their judgment and experience the best enabled to appreciate the effect of the proposed measure upon the native army.' The replies of these officers were received with the following results: five were opposed to all interference whatever with the practice, twelve were favourable to abolition but averse to absolute and direct prohibition under the authority of the Government, eight supported abolition by the indirect interference of magistrates and other public officers, while the remaining twenty-four advocated the total, immediate, and public suppression of the practice. But the most important and unanimous portion of the evidence furnished from these specially qualified witnesses was that affirming that the sepoy was far less interested than had been supposed in the practice of *satí*. The best information went to prove that it was almost unknown in the ranks of the Bengal army, and that any interest the sepoy felt in the matter must be indirect and probably remote. The chief peril attendant on the abolition of *satí* was dispelled when it became realised that it would not affect the favoured sepoy of the Bengal army in any of his practices or privileges. It is true that there was the more remote and contingent danger of irritating the high caste race from which that army was recruited; but this might reasonably be hoped to disappear by other means and by the natural effluxion of time. The main objection to legislative action, the risk upon which the Marquis of Hastings and others had laid such stress, was thus found to be not applicable in fact, and rather a figment of the imagination than a substantial reality.

Of the danger from any ebullition of popular antipathy in the Lower Provinces, where the practice of *satí* was most in vogue, Lord William Bentinck thought and wrote with accurate knowledge and proper scorn.

The people who were the chief upholders of *satí* were unwarlike and accustomed to submit without opposition to authority. Even had the abolition of *satí* been an unjust and unnecessary act, it would not have provoked any rebellious spirit among the races most devoted to the practice. But it was by the admission of every one an act called for in the interests of humanity, and only set on one side temporarily by responsible statesmen because of the perils it might entail to the British Government in India. The preliminary investigation set on foot by Lord William Bentinck showed that those perils had either been much exaggerated or were totally non-existent, and with the proof of their unreality disappeared the last objection to the required reform.

While the commission of officers referred to were diligently collecting information as to the opinion and feeling prevalent in the ranks of the native army, and recording their advice individually as to the mode of dealing with the practice, the hands of Lord William Bentinck were much strengthened by the support of the Nizámat Adálat, the Judges of which Court were well aware of the uselessness of the tentative measures taken to remove some of the most objectionable and repulsive features of *satí* In 1828, before the military officers had begun their work, the Report of the Nizámat Adálat placed on record the strong expression of the opinion of four out of its five Judges that the immediate abolition of the practice of *satí* was desirable, and that in their opinion it might be accomplished with safety. Twelve months later the fifth Judge came to the same conclusion, and the Report of the Court for 1829 was unanimous to the effect that *satí* could and should be permanently abolished.

The expression of such a strong and emphatic opinion in favour of the reform from the highest judicial tribunal in the land could not be ignored, and came as a welcome support to a Governor-General who was most anxious to settle the question in accordance with the dictates of humanity, if also in harmony with the requirements of safe government. Nor did the Judges stand alone in their expression of confidence as to the safety with which the abolition might be effected. What they said was fully borne out by the most experienced police authorities. The Superintendents of Police in both the Upper and Lower

Provinces stated in the strongest terms their opinion that the suppression of *satí* might be ordered without the least danger. Lord William Bentinck asserts that nine-tenths of the public functionaries in the interior were in favour of abolition. When these opinions were added to those recorded by the forty-nine officers to whom the Governor-General wrote, there resulted a general agreement on the part of the persons best qualified to speak that the abolition of *satí* was desirable on every ground, and that it might be so enacted without the risk of any popular disturbance or military discontent. It enabled Lord William Bentinck to express the hope to his Council that 'they will partake in the perfect confidence which it has given me of the expediency and safety of the abolition.'

The discussion of the matter in Council did not take long, and one month after Lord William Bentinck's Minute there appeared in the Calcutta Government Gazette of December 7, 1829, the Regulation, known as No. XVII, and dated December 4, 1829, 'declaring the practice of *satí*, or of burning or burying alive the widows of Hindus, illegal and punishable by the Criminal Courts.' The Regulation went on to state that the practice of *satí* is 'revolting to the feelings of human nature,' and 'nowhere enjoined by the religion of the people as an imperative duty.' It then summarises the previous efforts to deal with the evil, all of which had been barren of result, until at last the Government had been forced to come to the conclusion that there was no remedy left 'without abolishing the practice altogether.' This course was demanded by the 'paramount dictates of justice and humanity.'

Having decreed the abolition of *satí*, the practice of that rite was made a crime of culpable homicide, punishable with fine or imprisonment, or with both. The Court was not to be precluded from passing even a sentence of death, and, lastly, all persons were called upon under heavy penalties to give the authorities immediate information of any cases coming within their knowledge. The Regulation referred in the first place to the Presidency of Bengal alone, but in 1830 it was extended in different forms, rendered necessary by local requirements, to Madras and Bombay.

The result of the abolition of *satí* fully bore out the predictions made as to the degree of safety with which it could be accomplished. No public disorder followed the enactment. If there was any dissatisfaction it was carefully suppressed. The few disturbances caused by excited Bengalis were too insignificant to attract comment, and the only serious incident happened some years afterwards in a state in Central India, when on the death of the Rájá five of his wives were forcibly burned. If the Bengalis did not attempt anything so foreign to their nature as violent resistance, they endeavoured to fight the matter in the Courts, and a test case was submitted by them to the Privy Council in London.

Petitions to the King were drawn up, declaring that the abolition of *satí* was an infraction of the rights of the peoples of India, which we had bound ourselves to respect. But the weight of these was weakened by counter-petitions signed by eminent leaders of native opinion like Dwarakanath Tagore and Rammohun Roy, declaring that the resolution of Government was in harmony with their opinion and with the best interpretation of the Hindu religion.

When the case came before the Privy Council it was regarded and considered purely in its judicial aspect. The rival representatives of Hindu opinion neutralised each other, and although a feeling of reluctance to interfere in any shape or form with what might be considered a religious rite was very prevalent, the decision arrived at was based on legal arguments alone. The case was fully argued in June, 1832, and after careful consideration of the arguments advanced on both sides, the petition of the Hindu appellants was dismissed, and the act of the Government of India received a formal legal ratification. With regard to this case, Mr. Greville[1], who was Clerk of the Council, declares that 'the Court were half-hearted in the matter, but practically unanimous in thinking that the Governor-General's orders could not be set aside.'

Before the passing of the measure abolishing *satí*, the only criticism that was heard was based on the perils attendant upon such a step. But after it had

[1] Greville Memoirs, vol. ii. pp. 314–5.

been safely taken, the tendency became to minimise the importance of the measure and to disparage the fortitude and foresight which ensured its success. Expression is given to this feeling by Mr. Shore, who plays the part of candid friend to Lord William Bentinck in regard to several matters, and who seeks to diminish the value of the Regulation abolishing *satí*. He wrote in his 'Notes on Indian Affairs':—

> 'Regarding the *satí* question, Lord William Bentinck did not go far enough. In addition to abolishing that horrible rite he should have enacted some rules to provide for the maintenance of widows.'

But we may venture to assert that no one who takes a practical view of the passing of great reforms will endorse that criticism. Although Lord William Bentinck took every possible step to obtain beforehand the best information as to how his measure would be received by the Hindus, and although the result realised his expectations, it must be remembered that there was a possibility of the consequences proving very different, and it would have been a mark of incompetence as a statesman for Lord William Bentinck to have added unnecessarily to the risk of the success of his great reform by insisting that not only should the lives of widows be spared, but that they should be provided for at the expense of the family. All measures of reform must be progressive, and no single legislative act was ever sufficiently comprehensive to include all the points that might arise under it. In the matter of *satí* Lord William Bentinck aimed at 'washing out a foul stain upon British rule,' and in this object he was completely successful.

The quoting of Lord William Bentinck's own words on this matter suggests a few concluding remarks on the principles underlying our policy in India, which have as much force to-day as they had sixty years ago, when Indian reform was first taken seriously in hand by the abolition of *satí*. Non-interference with the practice of the natives was the first article of faith with the East India Company, which, while admitting in their fullest extent the services it rendered to the State, was, after all, a commercial body in its essence. And it may be freely admitted that the determination to show all possible respect and consideration to the practices and prejudices of the Indian population was, and still is, sound policy. But, after all, there is another side of the question. It may be difficult to draw up on paper the limits of toleration, and to declare beforehand the points at which active intervention should commence. But practical administrators should never have any difficulty in deciding when a Hindu practice must be considered a foul stain on British rule. It is unjustifiable from every point of view except religious bigotry, and impolitic in the extreme, to take steps which point to our desire to convert the Hindus and other Indian creeds to Christianity. Their religion should be as sacred in the eyes of those who govern them as it is in their own. When we refuse to recognise this truth, and act in contravention of it, we shall have gone far to the loss of our Indian Empire.

But respect and protection for the special religion of the Hindus cannot and must not allow us to be blind to acts which are in contravention of all religion, and opposed to the most clearly established rights of humanity. No religion can justify the sacrifice of innocent persons. A civilised Government is bound to protect them, or to lose its reputation. It was for that reason that, even if the Hindus had made the abolition of *satí* an excuse of revolt, we were bound to intervene for the protection of widows, guiltless of all offence, and led too often to an unwelcome as well as a cruel bier. The same considerations that drove Lord William Bentinck to action in 1829 have driven his successor, Lord Lansdowne, to pass a measure against the act of cruelty inseparable from child marriages.

The enlightened and educated Hindu must realise that the legislation directed against special acts of what can only be considered human cruelty, arising from ignorance sanctioned by long usage, does not injure his religion in the least. With the doctrine and the purely religious ceremonies of Hinduism, the Government of India has no more inclination or intention to meddle than it has with the creeds of the Muhammadans and the Parsis. But a solemn and imperative duty rests upon us to put an end to cruel and brutalising acts wherever committed under our jurisdiction, and for these we cannot allow either religion or long usage to be an excuse or a safeguard.

Minute by Lord William Bentinck, November 8th, 1829.

Whether the question be to continue or to discontinue the practice of *satí*, the decision is equally surrounded by an awful responsibility. To consent to the consignment year after year of hundreds of innocent victims to a cruel and untimely end when the power exists of preventing it is a predicament which no conscience can contemplate without horror. But, on the other hand, if heretofore received opinions are to be considered of any value, to put to hazard by a contrary course the very safety of the British Empire in India, and to extinguish at once all hopes of those great improvements—affecting the condition not of hundreds and thousands but of millions—which can only be expected from the continuance of our supremacy, is an alternative which even in the light of humanity itself may be considered as a still greater evil. It is upon this first and highest consideration alone, the good of mankind, that the tolerance of this inhuman and impious rite can in my opinion be justified on the part of the Government of a civilised nation. While the solution of this question is appalling from the unparalleled magnitude of its possible results, the considerations belonging to it are such as to make even the stoutest mind distrust its decision. On the one side, Religion, Humanity, under the most appalling form, as well as vanity and ambition—in short, all the most powerful influences over the human heart—are arrayed to bias and mislead the judgment. On the other side, the sanction of countless ages, the example of all the Mussulman conquerors, the unanimous concurrence in the same policy of our own most able rulers, together with the universal veneration of the people, seem authoritatively to forbid, both to feeling and to reason, any interference in the exercise of their natural prerogative. In venturing to be the first to deviate from this practice it becomes me to show that nothing has been yielded to feeling, but that reason, and reason alone, has governed the decision.

So far indeed from presuming to condemn the conduct of my predecessors, I am ready to say that in the same circumstances I should have acted as they have done. So far from being chargeable with political rashness, as this departure from an established policy might infer, I hope to be able so completely to prove the safety of the measures as even to render unnecessary any calculation of the degree of risk which for the attainment of so great a benefit might wisely and justly be incurred. So far also from being the sole champion of a great and dangerous innovation, I shall be able to prove that the vast preponderance of present authority has long been in favour of abolition. Past experience indeed ought to prevent me, above all men, from coming lightly to so positive a conclusion. When Governor of Madras I saw in the mutiny of Vellore the dreadful consequences of a supposed violation of religious customs upon the minds of the native population and soldiery. I cannot forget that I was then the innocent victim of that unfortunate catastrophe; and I might reasonably dread, when the responsibility would justly attach to me in the event of failure, a recurrence of the same fate. Prudence and self-interest would counsel me to tread in the footsteps of my predecessors. But in a case of such momentous importance to humanity and civilisation that man must be reckless of all his present or future happiness who could listen to the dictates of so wicked and selfish a policy. With the firm undoubting conviction entertained upon this question, I should be guilty of little short of the crime of multiplied murder if I could hesitate in the performance of this solemn obligation. I have been already stung with this feeling. Every day's delay adds a victim to the dreadful list, which might perhaps have been prevented by a more early submission of the present question. But during the whole of the present year much public agitation has been excited, and when discontent is abroad, when exaggerations of all kinds are busily circulated, and when the native army have been under a degree of alarm lest their allowances should suffer with that of their European officers, it would have been unwise to have given a handle to artful and designing enemies to disturb the public peace. The recent measures of Government for protecting the interests of the Sepoys against the late reduction of companies will have removed all apprehension of the intentions of Government; and the consideration of this circumstance having been the sole cause of hesitation on my part, I will now proceed, praying the blessing of God upon our counsels, to state the grounds upon which my opinion has been formed.

We have now before us two reports of the Nizámat Adálat, with statements of *satís* in 1827 and 1828, exhibiting a decrease of 54 in the latter year as compared with 1827, and a still greater proportion as compared with former years. If this diminution could be ascribed to any change of opinion upon the question produced by the progress of education or civilisation the fact would be most satisfactory, and to disturb this sure though slow process of self-correction would be most impolitic and unwise. But I think it may be safely affirmed that though in Calcutta truth may be said to have made a considerable advance among the higher orders; yet in respect to the population at large no change whatever has taken place, and that from these causes at least no hope of the abandonment of the rite can be rationally entertained. The decrease, if it be real, may be the result of less sickly seasons, as the increase in 1824 and 1825 was of the greater prevalence of cholera. But it is probably in a greater measure due to the more open discouragement of the practice given by the greater part of the European functionaries in latter years, the effect of which would be to produce corresponding activity in the police officers, by which either the number would be really diminished or would be made to appear so in the returns.

It seems to be the very general opinion that our interference has hitherto done more harm than good by lending a sort of sanction to the ceremony, while it has undoubtedly tended to cripple the efforts of magistrates and others to prevent the practice.

I think it will clearly appear from a perusal of the documents annexed to this Minute, and from the facts which I shall have to adduce, that the passive submission of the people to the influence and power beyond the law—which in fact and practically may be and is often exercised without opposition by every public officer—is so great that the suppression of the rite would be completely effected by a tacit sanction alone on the part of Government. This mode of extinguishing it has been recommended by many of those whose advice has been asked; and no doubt this in several respects might be a preferable course, as being equally effectual while more silent, not exciting the alarm which might possibly come from a public enactment, and from which in case of failure it would be easy to retreat with less inconvenience and without any compromise of character. But this course is clearly not open to Government, bound by Parliament to rule by law and not by their good pleasure. Under the present position of the British Empire, moreover, it may be fairly doubted if any such underhand proceeding would be really good policy. When we had powerful neighbours and had greater reason to doubt our own security, expediency might recommend an indirect and more cautious proceeding, but now that we are supreme my opinion is decidedly in favour of an open, avowed, and general prohibition, resting altogether upon the moral goodness of the act and our power to enforce it; and so decided is my feeling against any half measure that were I not convinced of the safety of total abolition I certainly should have advised the cessation of all interference.

Of all those who have given their advice against the abolition of the rite, and have described the ill effects likely to ensue from it, there is no one to whom I am disposed to pay greater deference than Mr. Horace Wilson. I purposely select his opinion because, independently of his vast knowledge of Oriental literature, it has fallen to his lot, as secretary to the Hindu College, and possessing the general esteem both of the parents and of the youths, to have more confidential intercourse with natives of all classes than any man in India. While his opportunity of obtaining information has been great beyond all others, his talents and judgment enable him to form a just estimate of its value. I shall state the most forcible of his reasons, and how far I do and do not agree with him.

1st. Mr. Wilson considers it to be a dangerous evasion of the real difficulties to attempt to prove that *satîs* are not 'essentially a part of the Hindu religion.' I entirely agree in this opinion. The question is not what the rite is but what it is supposed to be, and I have no doubt that the conscientious belief of every order of Hindus, with few exceptions, regard it as sacred.

2nd. Mr. Wilson thinks that the attempt to put down the practice will inspire extensive dissatisfaction. I agree also in this opinion. He thinks that success will only be partial, which I doubt. He does not imagine that the promulgated prohibition will lead to any immediate and overt act of insubordination, but that affrays and much agitation of the public mind must ensue. But he conceives that if once they suspect that it is the intention of the British Government to abandon this hitherto inviolate principle of allowing the most complete toleration in matters of religion that there will arise in the minds of all so deep a distrust of our ulterior designs that they will no longer be tractable to any arrangement intended for their improvement, and that the principle of a purer morality, as well as of a more virtuous and exalted rule of action, now actively inculcated by European education and knowledge, will receive a fatal check. I must acknowledge that a similar opinion as to the probable excitation of a deep distrust of our future intentions was mentioned to me in conversation by that enlightened native, Ram Mohun Roy, a warm advocate for the abolition of *satí* and of all other superstitions and corruptions engrafted on the Hindu religion, which he considers originally to have been a pure Deism. It was his opinion that the practice might be suppressed quietly and unobservedly by increasing the difficulties and by the indirect agency of the police. He apprehended that any public enactment would give rise to general apprehension, that the reasoning would be, 'While the English were contending for power they deemed it politic to allow universal toleration and to respect our religion, but having obtained the supremacy their first act is a violation of their profession, and the next will probably be, like the Muhammadan conquerors, to force upon us their own religion.'

Admitting, as I am always disposed to do, that much truth is contained in these remarks, but not at all assenting to the conclusions which, though not described, bear the most unfavourable import, I shall now inquire into the evil and the extent of danger which may practically result from this measure.

It must be first observed that of the 463 *satís* occurring in the whole of the Presidency of Fort William, 420 took place in Bengal, Behar, and Orissa, or what is termed the

Lower Provinces, and of these latter 287 in the Calcutta Division alone.

It might be very difficult to make a stranger to India understand, much less believe, that in a population of so many millions of people as the Calcutta Division includes, and the same may be said of all the Lower Provinces, so great is the want of courage and of vigour of character, and such the habitual submission of centuries, that insurrection or hostile opposition to the will of the ruling power may be affirmed to be an impossible danger. I speak of the population taken separately from the army, and I may add for the information of the stranger, and also in support of my assertion, that few of the natives of the Lower Provinces are to be found in our military ranks. I therefore at once deny the danger *in toto* in reference to this part of our territories, where the practice principally obtains.

If, however, security was wanting against extensive popular tumult or revolution, I should say that the Permanent Settlement, which, though a failure in many other respects and in its most important essentials, has this great advantage at least, of having created a vast body of rich landed proprietors deeply interested in the continuance of the British Dominion and having complete command over the mass of the people; and in respect to the apprehension of ulterior views, I cannot believe that it could last but for the moment. The same large proprietary body, connected for the most part with Calcutta, can have no fears of the kind, and through their interpretation of our intentions and that of their numerous dependents and agents, the public mind could not long remain in a state of deception.

Were the scene of this sad destruction of human life laid in the Upper instead of the Lower Provinces, in the midst of a bold and manly people, I might speak with less confidence upon the question of safety. In these Provinces the *satis* amount to forty-three only upon a population of nearly twenty millions. It cannot be expected that any general feeling, where combination of any kind is so unusual, could be excited in defence of a rite in which so few participate, a rite also notoriously made too often subservient to views of personal interest on the part of the other members of the family.

It is stated by Mr. Wilson that interference with infanticide and the capital punishment of Bráhmans offer a fallacious analogy with the prohibition now proposed. The distinction is not perceptible to my judgment. The former practice, though confined to particular families, is probably viewed as a religious custom; and as for the latter, the necessity of the enactment proves the general existence of this exception, and it is impossible to conceive a more direct and open violation of their Shasters, or one more at variance with the general feelings of the Hindu population. To this day in all Hindu states the life of a Bráhman is, I believe, still held sacred.

But I have taken up too much time in giving my own opinion when those of the greatest experience and highest official authority are upon our records. In the report of the Nizámat Adálat for 1828, four out of five of the Judges recommended to the Governor-General in Council the immediate abolition of the practice, and attest its safety. The fifth Judge, though not opposed to the opinions of the rest of the Bench, did not feel then prepared to give his entire assent. In the report of this year the measure has come up with the unanimous recommendation of the Court. The two Superintendents of Police for the Upper and Lower Provinces (Mr. Walter Ewer and Mr. Charles Barwell) have in the strongest terms expressed their opinion that the suppression might be effected without the least danger. The former officer has urged the measure upon the attention of Government in the most forcible manner. No documents exist to show the opinions of the public functionaries in the interior, but I am informed that nine-tenths are in favour of the abolition.

How, again, are these opinions supported by practical experience?

Within the limits of the Supreme Court at Calcutta not a *satí* has taken place since the time of Sir John Anstruther.

In the Delhi territory Sir Charles Metcalfe never permitted a *satí* to be performed.

In Jessore, one of the districts of the Calcutta Division, in 1824 there were 30 *satís;* in 1825, 16; in 1826, 3; in 1827 and in 1828 there were none. To no other cause can this be assigned than to a power beyond the law exercised by the acting magistrate, against which, however, no public remonstrance was made. Mr. Pigou has been since appointed to Cuttack, and has pursued the same strong interference as in Jessore, but his course, although most humane, was properly arrested, as being illegal, by the Commissioners. Though the case of Jessore is, perhaps, one of the strongest examples of efficacious and unopposed interposition, I really believe that there are few Districts in which the same arbitrary power is not exercised to prevent the practice. In the last work in the report of the Acting Commissioner (Mr. Smith) he states that in Gházipur in the last year sixteen, and in the preceding year seven, *satís* had been prevented by the persuasions, or, rather, it should be said, by the threats, of the Police.

Innumerable cases of the same kind might be obtained from the public records.

It is stated in the letter of the Collector of Gayá (Mr. Trotter), but upon what authority I have omitted to inquire, that the Peshwá (I presume he means the ex-Peshwá Bájí Ráo) would not allow the rite to be performed, and that in Tanjore it is equally interdicted. These facts, if true, would be positive proofs at least that no unanimity exists among the Hindus upon the point of religious obligation.

Having made inquiries, also, how far *satís* are permitted

in the European foreign settlements, I find from Dr. Carey that at Chinsurah no such sacrifices had ever been permitted by the Dutch Government. That within the limits of Chandarnagar itself they were also prevented, but allowed to be performed in the British territories. The Danish Government of Serampur has not forbidden the rite, in conformity to the example of the British Government.

It is a very important fact that, though representations have been made by the disappointed party to superior authority, it does not appear that a single instance of direct opposition to the execution of the prohibitory orders of our civil functionaries has ever occurred. How, then, can it be reasonably feared that to the Government itself, from whom all authority is derived, and whose power is now universally considered to be irresistible, anything bearing the semblance of resistance can be manifested? Mr. Wilson also is of opinion that no immediate overt act of insubordination would follow the publication of the edict. The Regulation of Government may be evaded, the Police may be corrupted, but even here the price paid as hush money will operate as a penalty, indirectly forwarding the object of Government.

I venture, then, to think it completely proved that from the Native population nothing of extensive combination, or even of partial opposition, may be expected from the abolition.

It is, however, a very different and much more important question how far the feelings of the Native army might take alarm, how far the rite may be in general observance by them, and whether, as in the case of Vellore, designing persons might not make use of the circumstances either for the purpose of immediate revolt or of sowing the seeds of permanent disaffection. Reflecting upon the vast disproportion of numbers between our Native and European troops, it was obvious that there might be, in any general combination of the forces, the greatest danger to the State, and it became necessary, therefore, to use every precaution to ascertain the impression likely to be made upon the minds of the native soldiery.

Before I detail to Council the means I have taken to satisfy my mind upon this very important branch of the inquiry, I shall beg leave to advert to the name of Lord Hastings. It is impossible but that to his most humane, benevolent, and enlightened mind this practice must have been often the subject of deep and anxious meditation. It was consequently a circumstance of ill omen and some disappointment not to have found upon the Records the valuable advice and direction of his long experience and wisdom. It is true that during the greater part of his administration he was engaged in war, when the introduction of such a measure would have been highly injudicious. To his successor, Lord Amherst, also, the same obstacle was opposed. I am, however, fortunate in possessing a letter from Lord Hastings to a friend in England upon *satis*, and from the following extract, dated 21 November, 1823, I am induced to believe that, had he remained in India, this practice would long since have been suppressed:—

'The subject which you wish to discuss is one which must interest one's feeling most deeply, but it is also one of extreme nicety when I mention that in one of the years during my administration of government in India about 800[1] widows sacrificed themselves within the Provinces comprised in the Presidency of Bengal, to which number I very much suspect that very many not notified to the magistrate should be added. I will hope to have credit for being acutely sensible to such an outrage against humanity. At the same time I was aware how much danger might attend the endeavouring to suppress forcibly a practice so rooted in the religious belief of the natives. No men of low caste are admitted into the ranks of the Bengal army. Therefore the whole of that formidable body must be regarded as blindly partial to a custom which they consider equally referrible to family honour and to point of faith. To attempt the extinction of the horrid superstition without being supported in the procedure

[1] There must be a mistake in the numbers stated.—W. B.

by a real concurrence on the part of the army would be distinctly perilous. I have no scruple to say that I did believe I could have carried with me the assent of the army towards such an object. That persuasion however arose from circumstances which gave me peculiar influence over the native troops[1].'

Lord Hastings left India in 1823. It is quite certain that the Government of that time were much more strongly impressed with the risk of the undertaking than is now very generally felt. It would have been fortunate could this measure have proceeded under the auspices of that distinguished nobleman, and that the State might have had the benefit of the influence which undoubtedly he possessed in a peculiar degree over the native troops. Since that period, however, six years have elapsed. Within the territories all has been peaceful and prosperous, while without, Ava and Bhartpur, to whom alone a strange sort of consequence was ascribed by public opinion, have been made to acknowledge our supremacy. In this interval experience has enlarged our knowledge, and has given us surer data upon which to distinguish truth from illusion, and to ascertain the real circumstances of our position and power. It is upon these that the concurring opinion of the officers of the civil and military services at large having been founded, is entitled to our utmost confidence.

I have the honour to lay before Council the copy of a circular addressed to forty-nine officers, pointed out to me by the Secretary to Government in the Military Department as being from their judgment and experience the best enabled to appreciate the effect of the proposed measure upon the native army, together with their answers. For more easy reference, an abstract of each answer is annexed in a separate paper and classed with those to the same purport.

It appears first that of those whose opinions are directly

[1] [This quotation has been separately given for convenience on a previous page.—*Ed.*]

adverse to all interference whatever with the practice the number is only five; secondly, of those who are favourable to abolition but averse to absolute and direct prohibition under the authority of the Government, the number is twelve; thirdly, of those who are favourable to abolition, to be effected by the indirect interference of magistrates and other public officers, the number is eight; fourthly, of those who advocate the total immediate and public suppression of the practice, the number is twenty-four.

It will be observed, also, of those who are against an open and direct prohibition, few entertain any fear of immediate danger. They refer to a distant and undefined evil. I can conceive the possibility of the expression of dissatisfaction and anger being immediately manifested upon this supposed attack on their religious usages, but the distant danger seems to me altogether groundless, provided that perfect respect continues to be paid to all their innocent rites and ceremonies, and provided also that a kind and considerate regard be continued to their worldly interests and comforts.

I trust, therefore, that the Council will agree with me in the satisfactory nature of this statement, and that they will partake in the perfect confidence which it has given me of the expediency and safety of the abolition.

In the answer of one of the military officers, Lieutenant-Colonel Todd, he has recommended that the tax on pilgrims should be simultaneously given up, for the purpose of affording an undoubted proof of our disinterestedness and of our desire to remove every obnoxious obstacle to the gratification of their religious duties. A very considerable revenue is raised from this head, but if it were to be the price of satisfaction and confidence to the Hindus and of the renewal of all distrust of our present and future intentions, the sacrifice might be a measure of good policy. The objections that must be entertained by all to the principle of the tax, which in England has latterly excited very great reprobation, formed an additional motive for the inquiry. I enclose the copy of a circular letter addressed to different individuals at present in charge of the district where the tax is collected, or who have had opportunities, from their local knowledge, of forming a good judgment upon this question. It will be seen that opinions vary, but upon a review of the whole my conviction is that in connection with the present measure it is inexpedient to repeal the tax. It is a subject upon which I shall not neglect to bestow more attention than I have been able to do. An abstract of these opinions is annexed to this minute.

I have now to submit for the consideration of Council the draft of a regulation enacting the abolition of *satís*. It is accompanied by a paper containing the remarks and suggestions of the Judges of the Nizámat Adálat. In this paper is repeated the unanimous opinions of the Court in favour of the proposed measure. The suggestions of the Nizámat Adálat are in some measure at variance with a principal object I had in view, of preventing collision between the parties to the *satí* and the officers of police. It is only in the previous processes, or during the actual performance of the rite, when the feelings of all may be more or less roused to a high degree of excitement, that I apprehend the possibility of affray or of acts of violence through an indiscreet and injudicious exercise of authority. It seemed to me prudent, therefore, that the police, in the first instance, should warn and advise, but not forcibly prohibit, and if the *satí*, in defiance of this notice, were performed, that a report should be made to the magistrate, who would summon the parties and proceed as in any other case of crime. The Indian Court appears to think these precautions unnecessary, and I hope they may be so, but in the beginning we cannot, I think, proceed with too much circumspection. Upon the same principle, in order to guard against a too hasty or severe a sentence emanating from extreme zeal on the part of the local judge, I have proposed that the case should only be cognizable by the Commissioners of circuit. These are, however, questions which I should wish to see discussed in Council. The other recommendations of the Court are well worthy of our adoption.

I have now brought this paper to a close, and I think I have redeemed my pledge of not allowing, in the consideration of this question, passion or feeling to have any part. I trust it will appear that due weight has been given to all difficulties and objections, that facts have been stated with truth and impartiality, that the conclusion to which I have come is completely borne out both by reason and authority. It may be justly asserted that the Government in this act will only be following, not preceding, the tide of public opinion long flowing in this direction; and when we have taken into consideration the experience and wisdom of that highest public tribunal, the Nizámat Adálat, who, in unison with our wisest and ablest public functionaries, have been year after year almost soliciting the Government to pass this act, the moral and political responsibility of not abolishing this practice far surpasses, in my judgment, that of the opposite course.

But discarding, as I have done, every inviting appeal from sympathy and humanity, and having given my verdict, I may now be permitted to express the anxious feelings with which I desire the success of this measure.

The first and primary object of my heart is the benefit of the Hindus. I know nothing so important to the improvement of their future condition as the establishment of a purer morality, whatever their belief, and a more just conception of the will of God. The first step to this better understanding will be dissociation of religious belief and practice from blood and murder. They will then, when no longer under this brutalising excitement, view with more calmness acknowledged truths. They will see that there can be no inconsistency in the ways of Providence, that to the command received as divine by all races of men, 'No innocent blood shall be spilt,' there can be no exception; and when they shall have been convinced of the error of this first and most criminal of their customs, may it not be hoped that others, which stand in the way of their improvement, may likewise pass away, and that thus emancipated from those chains and shackles upon their minds and actions, they may no longer continue, as they have done, the slaves of every foreign conqueror, but that they may assume their first places among the great families of mankind? I disown in these remarks, or in this measure, any view whatever to conversion to our own faith. I write and feel as a legislator for the Hindus, and as I believe many enlightened Hindus think and feel.

Descending from these higher considerations, it cannot be a dishonest ambition that the Government of which I form a part should have the credit of an act which is to wash out a foul stain upon British rule, and to stay the sacrifice of humanity and justice to a doubtful expediency; and finally, as a branch of the general administration of the Empire, I may be permitted to feel deeply anxious that our course shall be in accordance with the noble example set to us by the British Government at home, and that the adaptation, when practicable to the circumstances of this vast Indian population, of the same enlightened principles, may promote here as well as there the general prosperity, and may exalt the character of our nation.

W. C. BENTINCK.

November 8th, 1829.

CHAPTER VI

RENEWAL OF THE COMPANY'S CHARTER

ALTHOUGH the Charter of the East India Company was not renewed until the Governor-Generalship of Lord William Bentinck was drawing to a conclusion, the question of its renewal occupied so much attention during the whole of this period that it will be convenient to consider it now, notwithstanding that it is a little out of its chronological order. Lord William Bentinck's appointment as Governor-General was made with a special eye to the Charter debates in the British Parliament, and his success in imparting not merely an equilibrium to the finances but a higher tone to the administration of India, answered the expectations of his employers, and promoted their interests in the legislative assembly of the Empire. As it was quite certain that there would be changes in the extent of the privileges conferred by the Charter, the East India Company was naturally anxious to make out the best possible case for itself against the animadversions of its critics. Nor was it possible to ignore the fact that the impeachment of Warren Hastings had left as its legacy an uneasy feeling among English public men that we had acquired grave responsibilities as well as increased trade and dominion by our conquests in India, and that perhaps after all a commercial body, such as the East India Company, was not the best qualified to discharge them. The active, pacific, and reforming administration of Lord William Bentinck enabled the Company to make out a far better case than it could otherwise have done, and for this reason his name will be associated with what was in some respects the most important renewal of the Charter originally granted by Queen Elizabeth.

The renewal of that Charter had often before suggested the idea of political combat, but on no previous occasion were the critics of the East India Company more energetic and jubilant than on the eve of the long Parliamentary discussion which was to finally strip it of its little remaining commercial character. Many causes conduced to this result, but perhaps the most significant of them all was the prevalent inclination for reform, which, fortunately for the East India Company, spent its force on matters more intimately connected with our home affairs than the condition of our trade and empire in the East. Had the energy which was evident when a Select Committee was first asked for in 1829 lasted down to the autumn of 1833, when the Bill renewing the Charter was finally passed, there is every probability that the House of Commons would have been induced to declare that the Company had had its day, and that the time had arrived for the British Parliament to assume the direct control of India. The interest in the question steadily diminished with each succeeding session, and the Bill was finally discussed and carried in an empty and exhausted House. The apathy of the British Parliament, more than the splendour of the Company's achievements or the skill of its advocates, obtained for the East India Company the desired renewal of its political powers.

The Charter which was granted by Queen Elizabeth to the old India Company in 1600 had been frequently renewed, and for different periods and purposes. The original Charter conferred on the Company its rights for a period of fifteen years, but when James I granted another in 1609 the period was left indefinite. Ignoring the charters of the minor companies and associations which enjoyed the favour of Oliver Cromwell or the Stuarts, and confining our attention to the original India Company into which the rest were ultimately absorbed, we find that one of the first acts of Charles II after the Restoration was to grant the Company a fresh Charter, conferring upon it larger powers, including the right of making peace or war with any of the native states of India. This was the first introduction of what may be called the political element into the life of the East India Company, which had up to that point been a strictly commercial body.

The next renewal of the Charter was by William III in 1698. This has been called the foundation of all the privileges which the Company enjoyed down to its death in 1858. Four years later the Charter of union between the rival companies confirmed these privileges, and left the period of their enjoyment indefinite. In 1733 and again in 1766 the rights of the East India Company were brought under the notice of Parliament, and in 1773 its charter was renewed for the definite period of twenty years. This fact deserves remembrance, for this interval continued to be observed until the last renewal of the Charter in 1853. The renewal in 1793 was made without any modification, but that in 1813 decreed that the monopoly of the Company of trade with India should cease, and that commerce with that country should be thrown open. It also provided for an ecclesiastical establishment, with a bishop at Calcutta and archdeacons at Madras and Bombay. A still more important change had been effected by Pitt's India Bill of 1784, which created the Board of Control. This Board, of six members, supervised the acts of the Company, and served as an intermediary between the Government at home and in India.

The withdrawal of the E. I. Company's monopoly of trade with India in 1813 was followed by an expansion of English commerce in Eastern seas that led to a growing demand for the opening of the trade with China. This feeling was greatly strengthened by the very prevalent expectations among English merchants and manufacturers that trade with that empire would rapidly develop and prove most profitable—expectations, it may be observed, which have been only partially realised at the present day. In the course of the year 1829 petitions were presented to Parliament praying that the Charter might not be renewed, and that if renewed it should not carry with it a monopoly of Chinese trade. In the same session a Select Committee was moved for, but it was not until the following year that it was appointed on a Government motion, Lord Ellenborough moving it in the Lords and Sir Robert Peel in the Commons. The Government, however, distinctly disclaimed all intention of interfering in the matter, leaving it to the calm and dispassionate judgment of Parliament. The questions submitted to the Committee were of the most comprehensive character, and the inquiry necessarily covered a wide ground. As Wilson well says in his continuation of Mill's History:—

> 'The question, however important to the commerce of the Empire, was not confined to commercial interests; it involved the whole character of the Government of India, the mode in which it might best be administered for the prosperity and happiness of the people, the reputation of the Legislature, and the dignity and rights of the Crown.'

The instructions of the Committee stated that it was 'appointed to inquire into the present state of the affairs of the East India Company, and into the trade between Great Britain and China, and to report their observations thereon to the House.'

The course of the Committee did not run smooth. The death of George IV brought its labours, with the life of the House of Commons, to a sudden and precipitate close. Reappointed in February, 1831, the early dissolution of Parliament again led to its own breaking up, and although reconstituted in June its inquiries were once more cut short in October by the necessity for a fresh election. Finally reconstituted in January, 1832, its report was presented to Parliament in the following August, so that the whole of the winter recess was left for the careful consideration of the voluminous facts ascertained by the Committee. The information was interesting even when it was contradictory, but there is much reason to suppose that it did not affect the verdict of Parliament, which had already made up its mind on the two main practical points, the trade with China and the administration of India. No one expected the former to be continued, and, indifferent as the House of Commons was to Indian questions, it did not minimise their difficulty, and still shrank from the responsibility of dealing with them.

The important and practical consideration of the question was carried on by negotiations between the Government and the Court of Directors, which preceded the presentation of the Bill to Parliament. The first clause of the proposed Bill laid down that 'the China monopoly was to cease.' The pros and cons of that branch of the question were considered at some length. On the one hand it was alleged by the Government, on the strength of the report of the Select Committee, that the profit of the China trade, which annually exceeded one million sterling, was derived from a tax both unpopular and unjust, paid by the British consumer, and that this fact was proved by the lower prices paid for tea on the continent. It was also alleged that the costliness of the East India Company's establishment at Canton contributed to make the price of tea excessive. The Court disputed these statements, alleging that the lower prices on the continent were due to the inferiority of the article sold, and also that their profit from the trade had been much exaggerated. But although reiterating their view of the case, the Court did not persist in fighting a hopeless battle, and accepted the first clause abolishing the China monopoly in deference to public opinion, and merely stipulated for the short respite necessary to dispose of the stock which they were bound to keep on hand.

The second clause of the projected Bill proposed that the East India Company should be entrusted with the renewed political control of India. As it was quite clear that this concession was only made because the British Government was unprepared to accept the responsibility itself, it followed that the Company's best device to obtain increased commercial privileges was to feign reluctance to accept the great administrative responsibility of ruling India. In support of this reluctance, the Court was able to show that the revenues of India had not sufficed alone to defray all the expenses of governing it, and that the deficit had only been made good out of the profits of the commercial operations of the East India Company. It followed as a necessary consequence that if these operations were abandoned the deficiency would have to be made good from some other quarter, as every one connected with the Company was agreed that competition with private traders would be ruinous and out of the question. Practically speaking the whole question turned on this point, for although there was difference of opinion as to the extent to which the Indian revenues were deficient, and as to whether that deficiency was likely to prove permanent or not, there was complete agreement on the fact that the dividends on the Company's stock were paid not out of Indian revenue, but out of the profits of the China trade. If that trade were abolished it was essential to ascertain whence the Company was to procure its dividend, as it could not be expected to perform the onerous task of governing India without some tangible reward.

On the great subject of the deficiency of the Indian revenue some facts and figures will be useful and explanatory of the whole situation. From 1823–4 to 1828–9 the average annual deficit was not less than £2,878,000, and taking the longer period of 1814–5 to 1828–9 we find that the total deficiency was £19,400,000. These figures were the result of considering the Indian revenues as the sole financial resource of the East India Company, and testify to the fact that the Indian revenues alone were at that time unequal to the charge of governing the country by means of an European administration. The serious deficit proved to arise from the government of India had been met by a considerable allocation of the profits of trade to the task of administration, and by public loans guaranteed by the Company. It was not an unfair or unexpected demand for the East India Company to ask before accepting the political direction of India for some guarantee as to the funds required for the accompanying expense.

While there was no room for disputing the main fact, it by no means followed that all the contentions put forward in consequence of it by the Company were well founded. Its advocates made a great point of the question of the home remittances, which then amounted to three millions sterling, alleging that there would be much difficulty in providing for their punctual and satisfactory discharge. The *modus operandi* of the Company had been simply to purchase goods in India and China, and to dispose of them in the London market, applying the proceeds to the payment of the home charges. When the commercial department of the Company was to be closed it seemed to them that no alternative was left to what was, after all, a very primitive arrangement. The most experienced bankers and merchants had no difficulty in exposing the fallacy of this belief, and in showing that the transmission of the necessary funds by bills would be easy and efficacious; and it may be pointed out that this arrangement has worked well ever since, and is still in force.

The Company was also on weak ground when assuming that because the revenue of India was insufficient for its purposes in 1829 it must necessarily always be so. Lord William Bentinck himself proved that the argument was untenable by converting a deficit of one million into a surplus of two millions, and although that was due to the preservation of peace, and the surplus disappeared when the expense of war in Afghanistan and the Punjab had to be provided for, there was still little or no doubt that the revenues of India, properly husbanded and directed, were fully equal to meeting all legitimate demands, especially when we consider that Lord William Bentinck's policy in the matter of the Málwá opium had practically ensured a valuable contribution, paid for by the Chinese drug-consumer, to take the place of the alleged payment to the Company by the English tea-drinker. Moreover no allowance was made for the effects of economy and the wide scope for developing the resources of India, which first began to taste the fruits of internal peace after the campaigns of Lord Hastings. On an impartial consideration of the question it must be allowed that the Company signally failed to prove its contention, that the resources of India must be unequal to the task of its government.

But as has been pointed out, the question of the dividend of the proprietors of the Company was apart from that of the administration of India, and on this subject it could reasonably claim every consideration. As the fight finally resolved itself into deciding what this should be, it is only necessary to summarise here the arrangement come to. The first proposition of the Government was, that the payment of the dividends to the proprietors should be regarded as an annuity chargeable on the territorial revenue of India, and redeemable after a period to be decided, and at the option of Parliament, by a payment of £100 for every five guineas of annuity. The total of the annuities amounted to £630,000 a year, and it was proposed that all the Company's commercial assets[1] should be converted into money, with which a sufficient amount of Indian territorial debt should be purchased to produce an income of £630,000 a year. In other words, what was proposed was an act of substitution, the revenue of India accepting the responsibility of paying the interest on the Company's stock, and the Company assigning its possessions to the reduction of India's liabilities by a similar amount, so that there should result no addition to the burden borne by the taxpayers of that country.

As the possessions of the Company would produce a sum sufficient for the payment of the annual dividend or for the redemption of the principal at twenty years' purchase, and as its right to its

[1] These were estimated by the Company at not less than £21,103,000, but as £8,428,000 were questionable assets, the net total was £12,675,900, which at 5 per cent. would have produced £630,000 a year.

commercial assets could hardly be disputed, it followed that the Government's proposition was not received with much approval. But the Government knew its strength and the weakness of the Company, and it brought all the pressure it possessed to bear on the Court of Directors. In reply to the statement of the value of the Company's property, it replied that the proper valuing and realisation of its possessions would take several years, and that the renewal of the Charter had to be settled one way or the other in a few months. If the Charter was to be renewed at all the Company must accept their view of the position. Intimidated by this argument the Court gave way, and agreed to the suggested transfer between commercial and territorial claims if the Government undertook to arrange that some collateral security should be provided for the payment of its dividend. Even to this suggestion, which was highly natural under the circumstances, the Government gave only a reluctant consent. In addition to the scheme already provided, it was arranged that the sum of £1,300,000 should be taken from the commercial assets, invested in British Government stock, and with accumulated interest should form a fund that was to go on increasing until it had reached twelve millions, when any further augmentation was to cease. After considerable discussion and after a meeting of the proprietors of the Company to ratify the action of the Directors, the Government was induced to increase the sum assigned under this arrangement to two millions, and with that alteration the arrangement described was carried out.

The history of these negotiations and the voluminous correspondence were placed before the Court of Proprietors at two general meetings held in March and April, 1833. At the latter, a series of resolutions were moved by Sir John Malcolm, the greatest Anglo-Indian of the day, approving the conduct and proposals of the Directors, and recommending that the terms of the Government should be accepted. The six resolutions stipulated in their order (1) that the Company should assent to conduct the government of India at the sacrifices demanded, provided they were furnished with sufficient powers, and that their pecuniary rights and claims were adjusted by a fair and liberal compromise; (2) reiterating the financial arrangement described for providing a collateral security; (3) that the administration of India should be given for a period of not less than twenty years; (4) that all measures of expense should originate with the Directors, subject to the control of the India Board; (5) that the Company should have some means of attracting publicity, through Parliament or otherwise, to its views, in any dispute it might have with the India Board; and (6) that the Court should retain sufficient power over the commercial assets to enable them to provide for the discharge of all obligations, and also for compensation to such of the commercial officers and servants of the Company as might be affected by the new arrangements.

The discussion on these resolutions occupied seven days, but in the end they were carried by the large majority of 477 to 52. The complaisance of the Court was rewarded by certain concessions on the part of the Ministers, the principal of which has already been noted in the augmentation of the fund from £1,300,000 to £2,000,000. They also withdrew the veto they had proposed for the India Board on the subject of the recall of Governors and military commanders—a proposition which had struck at the self-respect of the Company, and threatened to reduce its authority to a mere shadow. Most of the other suggestions were adopted in accordance with the views of the Company, and a Bill was drafted upon them and submitted in June to the two Houses of Parliament. The debate in the House of Commons calls for no notice. It was distinctly poor, and unworthy of the magnitude of the subject—if one brilliant speech by Macaulay be excepted. Mr. Charles Grant, afterwards Lord Glenelg, apologised to the House for asking its attention to matters at such a distance, and it was to empty benches and an uninterested audience that the scheme was unfolded for entrusting the Company with another twenty years' lease of the government of India. An attempt was made in Committee to contract the period of extension from twenty to ten years, but the precedents from 1773 were too strong to justify the reduction. The Bill was finally read in the House of Commons at the end of July, and sent up to the House of Lords.

The debate in the Upper Chamber was, as is so often the case in dealing with matters of imperial importance, more worthy of a Bill which was deciding not merely the fate of the two hundred millions of India, but the destiny of the most famous trading company the world had ever known, and which had made its achievements a part of English history. It was introduced by the Marquis of Lansdowne, the Nestor of the Whig party, supported by Lord Ripon, and approved by the Marquis Wellesley on the statement of Lord Lansdowne, but strenuously opposed on various grounds by Lord Ellenborough and the Duke of Wellington, who recorded his views of the great Company as he had known it in the days of Assaye and Argaum. The Court of Proprietors of the East India Company was again convened in August to express its approval of the Bill as passed by the House of Commons. After further discussion it acquiesced in the arrangement by a vote of 173 to 64, the reduced numbers showing the diminished interest of the Company itself in its fate, which the majority of the Proprietors may have considered already decided. On 20th of August the Bill received the royal assent, thus completing the arrangements for what was nominally the last but one, but in all important essentials the last, renewal of the Charter granted by Queen Elizabeth 233 years before.

In the course of the debate in the House of Lords the Marquis of Lansdowne referred in eloquent words to the good service Lord William Bentinck had rendered in India, to whose 'vigour and judgment,' he said, it was due that the expenses of that country had been reduced to such a point as to show that its government could be carried on by means of its own revenue apart from any advantage of trade. The admission of natives to a larger share in the administration, and the unrestricted entrance of Europeans into the country, with rights of domicile, pointed to an increased economy and development, and those innovations had no more consistent or powerful advocate than the Governor-General, who saw in them the only way of establishing an equilibrium between revenue and expenditure in India. His direct participation in the renewal of the Charter does not transpire, although his indirect influence upon its fortunes cannot be doubted. His economies and his confident belief that the Indian territorial revenue could bear the whole cost of administration inspired, on the one hand, the Government with its main reasons for entertaining the same belief, and on the other, the East India Company with an additional motive for accepting and clinging to the government of the country when there seemed no pecuniary advantage to be derived from it. At the same time, the character of his administration had unquestionably enhanced the reputation of the English government in India, and had reached a standard beyond which the most zealous advocate of the rights of India could not at the time aspire. Yet the only part Lord William Bentinck publicly played with regard to the renewal of the Charter was to issue a notice in the *Calcutta Gazette*, 'calling for a general illumination and a display of fireworks to celebrate the renewal of the Charter,' when the news reached India in October, 1833.

If the only verdict possible about the renewal of the Indian Charter for another term of twenty years in 1833 is that the result was a foregone conclusion, in that the Company could not hope to retain the monopoly of the China trade, and that the Government were resolved not to accept the administration of India, we still must regard it as a landmark in our connexion with the great Indian dependency which places England at the head of the empires of the world. The most unfriendly critic of the East India Company cannot deny that it had done its country excellent service. It had increased the trade of the nation in every quarter of the Eastern continent. The skill and determination of its representatives had driven a powerful rival from the field in France, a service especially valuable at a time when on the continent French arms were more fortunate than ours. In the blackest days of the American rebellion there never failed to come some cheering news from India, reviving the courage of the nation, and proving that the power of winning battles had not departed. The successes of the Peninsula were matched and heightened in their effect by the long succession of victories against some of the most formidable rulers and races of Hindustán that were achieved under

Wellesley and Hastings. In short, for the better part of a century the Company had provided the nation with the material for the greatest satisfaction in adding alike to its self-respect and financial prosperity. There would have been marked ingratitude if, without any cause shown, the country had come to a sudden and arbitrary conclusion that the Company should cease to exist.

Moreover the Company had shown its full intention to meet the loftier expectations formed by English public opinion as to our duties towards the inhabitants of India. Lord William Bentinck was sent out as a reforming Governor-General, and he instituted many reforms. If the British Parliament had taken over the control of the country it could not have done more for the people than he did. The progress of reform is necessarily slow, and whether the Crown or the Company exercised authority, there were the common obligations of government which could not be evaded by either. Lord William Bentinck's rule was conterminous with one of the brief periods of internal and external peace prior to the Mutiny. He turned it to the best possible account by introducing necessary economies, by carrying out essential reforms, by spreading education, and lastly by introducing the natives to a share in the work of administration. The Company which sanctioned these measures shared in their credit, and it would have been highly inconsistent, as well as ungrateful, to decree the death of a great institution at the very moment that it was giving fresh evidence of its worthiness to live.

CHAPTER VII

Internal Affairs

We may now take a comprehensive view and give a brief descriptive account of the general administration of India by Lord William Bentinck. Under this head we have to consider the always delicate and important relations that must subsist between the central Government and the semi-independent States of India, and although his rule was pacific in a marked degree, Lord William Bentinck had to arrange more than one question of difficulty with them. We may also record in chronicle form some of those passages and events in the daily life of his government that seem to possess more than ephemeral interest. Excluding external relations and matters of foreign policy, which will necessarily form the subject of a separate chapter, in this we may attempt to describe the general course of his administration, apart from his three great reforms, in regard to *thagí*, *satí*, and education.

One of his earliest measures was to pass a Government resolution forbidding the presentation or receipt of official and other presents by servants of the

Company. The practice was in established accordance with Eastern usage, but it had led to abuses and was thought to be incompatible with the dignity of the supreme Government. This reform held with regard to the civil service the same relation as the reduction of batta did to the army. It was intended to reduce the perquisites to which the Anglo-Indian official had been accustomed under the laxer system in force when the Company was a purely commercial association, and when nobody thought of closely criticising the conduct of its agents. At the same time Lord William Bentinck received the most precise instructions from the Directors to pursue a policy of non-intervention with the native States generally, and to leave the chiefs to follow their own ways. The intentions of the Directors were good, and the principle of the new policy sound, but its application at that particular moment was premature. The native rulers had not been stimulated by our example and exhortations to renewed efforts to purify their administration, and when they found that the very slight check we exercised was to be relaxed they not unnaturally relapsed into their old ways. The application of the policy, rather than the policy itself, proved unfortunate, and entailed in most cases a more active intervention than would have been the case if it had never been withdrawn. But for this the responsibility did not rest with Lord William Bentinck, whose instructions were as precise and positive in this as they had been on the subject of batta.

The control which the East India Company had established over the majority of the native States, and which was based on political and financial reasons rather than administrative, was in no instance more vigorously applied than in that of Haidarábád, the state ruled by the Nizam of the Deccan. From an early period of our presence in Southern India as a militant nation, the Nizam of Haidarábád had been our closely attached and almost constant ally. There had been one period of hesitation, when led away by hostile advisers and by the belief that an army disciplined by Frenchmen might be a match for that created by the English, he opposed us in arms, but the incident was a brief and passing one, and did not produce any durable impression on an alliance which held good during the struggles with the Maráthás and with Haidar Ali and his son Tipú in Southern India. The obligation to maintain a considerable contingent force at our disposal imposed a severe strain on the financial resources of the Nizam, and as these resources were not wisely dispensed or carefully husbanded, it happened that the payments often fell into arrear, and the disorganised condition of the Haidarábád exchequer even raised a fear lest they might fail altogether. It must not be supposed that the arrangement referred to was one-sided. If the English Government was benefited by the support of the financial and military resources of Haidarábád, the Nizam was saved by the English arms from being annihilated by the Maráthás at one time, and by the

Muhammadan power of Mysore at another. The arrangement may be fairly represented as having been mutually advantageous. With the view of ensuring greater efficiency in the Nizam's service, British officers were introduced into it, and controlled the assessment of land and the collection of taxes during the life of Nizam Sikander Jah.

In May, 1829, Sikander Jah died and was succeeded by his son, Nazir-ud-Daulat. In writing to express his condolences on the death of the Nizam, Lord William Bentinck offered the new ruler his good wishes on 'assuming the sovereignty of Haidarábád,' and he also notified 'the intention of Government to revise the heretofore objectionable style of correspondence between the heads of the two Governments.' On July 21 Nazir-ud-Daulat wrote asking the Governor-General to order the discontinuance of the check and control exercised by British officers. One month later the Governor-General replied, granting this request and withdrawing his representatives, and in October the Nizam was left to carry out his sovereign[1] pleasure in his own way. Curiously enough the Nizam, having got rid of English officials, presented a request to the Governor-General to allow him to raise a personal body-guard of fifty English soldiers, but he was induced to withdraw his request. The administration of the finances of Haidarábád did

[1] It will be noted that the term 'sovereignty' was only used in corresponding with the Nizam among all the princes of India. He was treated more as an ally than a feudatory.

not improve when the Nizam was left to his own discretion and the advice of Chandu Lall—a minister who thought more of exhibiting the power and wealth of his master by a lavish and ostentatious expenditure than of the real interests of the people. In the official records there are frequent references to his 'petty shifts and modes' of raising revenue—a course which resulted after his death in the Indian Government taking over in the time of Lord Dalhousie the Berar districts and applying their revenue to the discharge of the Nizam's obligations towards itself.

If the harmony of our relations with the largest of the native states was undisturbed, Lord William Bentinck had more cause for anxiety in regard to the affairs of two other states in Southern India, viz. Mysore and Coorg.

In Mysore the evil arose from maladministration. After the overthrow and death of Tipú Sultán at Seringapatam, we revived the former Hindu *régime* in the person of a descendant of the old Mahárájás, and we gave him as minister and adviser, Purnea, one of the ablest of Indian statesmen. When that minister retired in 1811 he left the government in a flourishing condition. The finances were on a sound basis, and the people were contented and happy. The new minister, Linga Ráj, had neither his ability nor his virtue. The exchequer was soon depleted, the people were burdened with taxation, and after twenty years of misgovernment they were ripe for revolt. The exhortations of the Resident, and a personal visit by the Governor of Madras, Sir Thomas Munro, brought promises of amendment and postponed the day of reckoning. But the extortions of the tax-gatherers were resumed after a little time, and the people refusing to submit, broke out in open rebellion and killed several of the Mahárájá's officers. In the province of Nagar the ráyats rose *en masse*, and began what might be called a peasants' war.

The Mysore army, although drilled by English officers, was unable to crush the movement, and a strong force of Madras troops had to be sent against the insurgents. At the same time it was announced that their grievances would be considered in a lenient spirit if they desisted from opposition, and the presence of English officers established confidence in the good faith of this offer. The excesses of the Mahárájá had so completely alienated public confidence that no reliance was placed on the offers made on paper to grant the peasants what they justly demanded. The people remained under arms, and although no fighting actually took place, it was evident that the only way to put an end to the disorders was to incorporate Mysore for a time with the British dominion. The Mahárájá was deposed under clauses in the treaty of 1799, and assigned a place of residence and a pension. An English Commissioner assumed the control of the administration, and in the course of a little time tranquillity and prosperity returned to the province. Mysore continued to enjoy the advantages of English administration down to 1881, when the descendant of the deposed Mahárájá was reinstalled, and is the present ruler of that province.

The second state with which interference became necessary was Coorg. The Rájá, whose excesses could only be explained on the supposition that he was out of his mind, refused to hold any relations with us whatever, and plotted to our disadvantage in Mysore and elsewhere. At last our patience was exhausted, and after a proclamation was issued declaring that 'the conduct of the Rájá had rendered him unworthy of the friendship and protection of the British Government,' war was declared against him. Lord William Bentinck, who happened to be staying at Utakamand at the time, assumed the personal direction of the campaign. His arrangements left no room for criticism on the ground of incompleteness or over-confidence. Four divisions were entrusted with the invasion of the difficult country of Coorg.

Although an ample force was employed in the operations, the invasion of Coorg was not attended with conspicuous military success, and it seemed likely to prove a very tedious business, when fortunately the Rájá, disheartened by the loss of his capital, surrendered himself a voluntary prisoner. He was deposed from power, assigned a residence at Benares and a pension, and Coorg, with the tacit acquiescence of the people themselves, as they at once desisted from hostility, became British territory.

The area of local disturbances covered the whole of India, but it was only in the two cases named that provinces had to be brought under direct British control. With the King of Delhi himself (who still retained the name of the Great Mogul) and with the ruler of Oudh there were constant bickerings and differences. The King of Delhi, who from being the patron had become the dependant of the Company, was dissatisfied with the amount of his allowance, and finding that there was no hope of obtaining what he wished from the authorities in India, he adopted as a possible remedy the unusual course of sending a special emissary to England, and he selected for this work Rammohun Roy, a Bráhman of great intelligence and attainments. The mission was abortive inasmuch as the English Government refused to recognise it, and the Governor-General was naturally irritated by a proceeding which seemed to aim at overriding his authority. The murder of Mr. Fraser, the Political Commissioner at Delhi, by a discontented chief, produced much excitement in that city, which was greatly increased when the criminal was brought to trial and hanged for his crime like an ordinary offender. These passages furnish evidence of the disorganised condition of affairs in the capital of Bábar's dynasty. The remembrance of departed power was always present to add bitterness to the existing financial embarrassment, and there is nothing surprising in the end having come twenty-five years later in the Mutiny.

At the other great Muhammadan capital of India, Lucknow, the state of affairs was still worse, and it was distinctly aggravated by the knowledge that, under the new policy, the Governor-General left the native rulers a free hand in appointing or getting rid of their ministers. The King of Oudh ruling during Lord William Bentinck's term of power had, as heir to the throne, been on terms of hostility with his father's minister, a man of considerable ability, known by his title of Motamid-ud-Daulat. On his father's death he pretended to sink his differences, and to take Motamid into his favour, but this was due rather to fear of the English Resident than to his own inclination. As soon as he realised that the Resident's hands were tied by his new instructions, he dismissed Motamid from office, and began a system of legal persecutions, which undoubtedly shortened the life of that official. The British Government, which had declared its fixed intention to stand aside, was insensibly drawn into the struggle, and the Resident refused to transact business with the incompetent and unworthy ministers by the aid of whom the King sought to carry on the administration. Against its own declared intentions, the Indian Government was thus drawn into controlling the King in his choice of a minister, and in the result the King was obliged to send for a former diwán and reinstate him in power.

The reforms set on foot by this minister, Mahdi Ali, arrested the downward descent of Oudh; but time was necessary for him to restore so thoroughly disorganised a State to anything approaching prosperity, and the King took pleasure in thwarting the best arrangements of his minister. The Resident reported that in his opinion there was no remedy for the evil but for us to assume the control of the State for a certain period, and Lord William Bentinck paid a special visit to Lucknow in 1831 to inform the King by word of mouth, and by a written despatch, that his territories must be better governed, or we should be compelled to annex them and depose him from power. Unfortunately we did not follow up this step by consistent action. For a brief space the King was impressed by the action of the Governor-General, but when Mahdi Ali appealed to the Resident for support it was refused on the plea of non-intervention, with the consequence that all his good intentions were never realised. At the same time that obedience was thus paid to the orders of the Directors, the Governor-General showed by his own action, and by the despatches he continually sent home recommending vigorous intervention in Oudh in the event of no amelioration taking place in its government, that the only remedy for maladministration in the native States was the vigilant supervision of the supreme authority, which his instructions forbade him to exercise. The vindication of Lord Dalhousie's annexion policy in 1856 would be found in the despatches of Lord William Bentinck in 1831 and 1832 on the subject of the internal condition of Oudh.

The gravest of all these minor disturbances occurred

in the Rájput state of Jaipur. In the time of Lord Amherst we had been compelled to intervene in the most energetic manner in the affairs of that state. The Indian Government not only appointed a permanent Resident, but banished an official named Jota Rám, who exercised a pernicious influence over the mother of the young Rájá. Although expelled from the state the influence of Jota Rám remained undiminished, and his faction formed the most powerful and energetic body in Jaipur. They spared no effort to discredit the minister who acted as Jota Rám's successor and to embarrass the British Resident. They succeeded so well in their machinations that the British Resident felt obliged to recommend the removal of the minister as the step most likely to restore tranquillity to Jaipur. For a time the Ráni was content to carry on the government by means of some of his creatures; but encouraged by her success she at last demanded that Jota Rám should be allowed to return and resume his post. With this request the Government of India also thought it well to comply. The success of the Ráni in her dealings with the English did not extend to her relations with the thákurs, or nobles of the State, who feigned no respect for a woman-regent, and who regarded Jota Rám as an adventurer.

The result of the conflict between the Ráni and the thákurs was that the former was continued in the regency, but this arrangement was not concluded until Sir Charles Metcalfe threw the weight of his personal influence into the scale in support of a pacific settlement. Much of the antipathy of the thákurs was due to the apprehension that the young Rájá had been made away with, and the production of the youthful ruler went far to allay the suspicions of his feudatories, and sufficed to procure for the Rání a bare majority of votes when the British Resident submitted to the nobles of Jaipur the question of her retaining the regency or not. Among the most pathetic incidents of English history in India is the sudden appearance of the Rájá—a child of eight years old, and the representative of a family whose origin is lost in antiquity—from behind the pardah, and his throwing himself, with touching confidence in the justice and sympathy of English authority, into the arms of Sir Charles Metcalfe, and begging there protection for himself and respect for his mother. To such an appeal there could only be one answer, and the conclave of nobles ratified the unexpressed wishes of the British representative.

Such was the position of affairs in Jaipur when Lord William Bentinck became Governor-General. It is not surprising to find that the new arrangement did not work satisfactorily, and that Jota Rám on his restoration to office behaved worse than he had done before. His one thought was to enrich himself as rapidly as possible at the expense of the peasant; but at the same time he did not conceal his animosity to those thákurs who had voted against the Rání, and he endeavoured to injure them in every way he could.

The guarantee of the British Government sufficed to preserve a hollow truce among the contending parties, but it was futile to pacify the unpaid soldiery, who had to be bribed into good-humour. The thákurs remained aloof and defiant, and the elevation of Jota Rám to the post of minister with the sanction of the British Government did not effect that improvement which was expected from this fresh accession of dignity.

Jota Rám was encouraged by his success to proceed to extremities against the thákurs. He curtailed their privileges, and attempted to substitute his own troops for theirs in the garrisoning of certain strongholds. This step provoked a civil war in 1830, and as the non-intervention theory was then in vogue the rival parties were left for a time to fight out their quarrel without our assistance or supervision. Such fighting as took place was of a desultory and uncertain character. It was only when Jota Rám menaced the territory of some of the thákurs whom we had guaranteed in their possessions that anything of a decisive nature took place. In face of the threat of a British force he was compelled to abandon the intention of appropriating the territory of some of the principal nobles. Baffled in this project he had recourse to other designs, in the midst of which, however, he lost the assistance of the Rání, who died in 1834. This event proved the beginning of more serious complications in Jaipur, for a few months later the young Rájá himself died, and it was strongly suspected from poison.

As may be imagined, this event greatly increased the indignation and excitement of the thákurs, who at once proceeded to Jaipur at the head of their armed retainers. Jota Rám offered to resign, and Major Alves, the Political Agent, was ordered to Jaipur to superintend the new arrangements necessary for the government of that state. It was quite clear that Jota Rám's offer was insincere, and that he would not resign his power without an effort to retain it; but the lengths to which he would go for the sake of ambition were only half suspected. His plot was marked by equal astuteness and audacity. He endeavoured to divert suspicion from himself at the same time that he had recourse to violent measures. By raising a popular disturbance on the very day of the Political Agent's arrival, and by hiring assassins to murder the English officers, he hoped to embroil the thákurs with the Government, and that he might be brought back to power through their being discredited.

The first part of his plot succeeded admirably. His emissaries raised a public disturbance; the assassins wounded the Agent, whose assistant, Mr. Blake, was killed by the mob, and in the midst of the disorder and alarm some thought that Jota Rám was the only person who could restore order. Unfortunately for him the assassin had been taken prisoner, and confessed that his instigators were Jain bankers, connected by blood and interest with Jota Rám. Jota Rám and his brother were arrested and brought to trial. They were both sentenced to death, but this penalty was commuted to imprisonment for life in British territory. The affairs of Jaipur were finally adjusted by the Council of Regency for the new Rájá (who was a mere child) being placed under the protection of a British Resident stationed permanently at the capital. Thus ended in the full assertion of our power the long period of confusion which had disturbed the most important of the Rájput states during ten years, and it would have been better for it and for us if that step had been taken at a much earlier period.

Our relations with the other native states of India were not without their gratifying features. Among these may be cited the refusal of the Mahárájá of Patiála to accept interest on a loan of twenty lakhs which he had very opportunely made to us. The same chief also sold to us for another tract of territory the remainder of the district of Simla, which was then beginning to be regarded as the most convenient sanitarium in India, and the proper headquarters of the Government during the hot weather. Our connexion with the place which is now so famous in Anglo-Indian life was not very old in the time of Lord William Bentinck. A portion of the hill on which it stands was retained by us after the war with Nepál in 1815–6. An English officer erected the first residence (a thatched, wooden cottage) there in 1819, and three years later this building was converted into a substantial house. In 1826 a small settlement had sprung up, to which the name of Simla was given, and in 1827 Lord Amherst was the first Governor-General to pay it a visit. In 1830 the remainder of the hill was obtained from the Mahárájá of Patiála in the manner described; and thenceforward, irregularly at first, but in the end with unfailing punctuality, the Government of India moved its headquarters to that pleasant resort on the slope of the Himálayas in the hot season of every year.

Simla was not the only hill sanitarium acquired during the time of Lord William Bentinck. One of his last acts was to purchase from the Rájá of Sikkim the site on which Dárjíling stands. After the war with the Gúrkhas in 1816 we restored that district, which they had seized, to the Rájá; and it was not until 1835 that we acquired by purchase the territory which was known until the other day as British Sikkim. Lord William Bentinck thus established the two best-known hill stations and sanitaria in Northern India.

One of the chief characteristics of Lord William Bentinck was his desire to see things for himself. Certainly no English ruler of India had visited so many parts of the peninsula. In the first six months of his Eastern residence he visited Burma, then recently annexed. Every summer saw him on tour, and when the accommodation of Simla was found to be insufficient for the requirements of a headquarter staff he proceeded to Utakamand, the sanitarium of

Madras. It was in some degree due to this habit of seeing things for himself that he obtained the reputation among Anglo-Indian officials, which finds expression in the pages of Shore, of being 'very suspicious and obstinate.' Indeed, all that somewhat acrid critic can find to say in his favour is that 'under Lord William Bentinck's administration the foundation of much solid improvement has been laid in India'—a grudging and unworthy summary of one of the most brilliant periods of reform in the history of the English in India.

Reference has been made to the fact that Lord William Bentinck found the Indian exchequer with a deficit of one million, and that he left it with a surplus of two millions. This was not the only financial difficulty with which he had to cope. Calcutta passed through a grave commercial crisis in the year 1833, when with hardly a sign of warning the five principal mercantile firms of that city failed. Their liabilities, which amounted to several millions, inflicted a most serious and much felt loss on the Company's servants who, attracted by a higher rate of interest, had deposited their savings with them. The cause of their downfall seems to have been their excessive expenditure, with a view of competing with the numerous rivals who appeared on the scene after the first withdrawal of the Company's commercial privileges. The effects of this keen competition were aggravated by the slow development of Indian trade, which did not increase in the manner expected, and which was in the end only stimulated by the introduction of steam navigation. That event came too late to avert the crash which destroyed the merchant princes of Calcutta, and the Government was helpless to avert it, or thought more of itself profiting by the occasion. Its efforts to borrow money had never previously succeeded when offering less than five per cent., but Lord William Bentinck was quick to see the opportunity furnished by the discredit of the private firms, and brought out in 1834 a four per cent. loan, which was very readily taken up. The winding up of the affairs of the house of Palmer and Co., of Haidarábád, which had failed in the time of Lord Amherst, produced much litigation during the Governor-Generalship of Lord William, and constituted another commercial incident of importance which should be mentioned, although space is not available to enter into the details of an exceedingly intricate and delicate matter. It is curious to note that one portion of the business, that relating to the claims of the representatives of Sir William Rumbold, who was a partner in the firm, was only settled a short time ago by the considerate and generous action of the present reigning Nizam.

In October, 1833, Lord William Bentinck assumed the command of the army on the retirement of Sir Edward Barnes, and thus combined the functions of Commander-in-Chief and Governor-General. This union of the highest civil and military posts had occurred on two previous occasions, in 1786 when the

Marquis Cornwallis held both offices, and again in 1813 in the person of the Marquis of Hastings.

Mention should not be omitted of Lord William Bentinck's 'magnificent hospitality,' to use the words of Mr. Greville. He was the first English ruler to entertain on a large scale, and under his auspices the breakfasts and receptions at Government House became a recognised function for simplifying the task of administration and for establishing social relations between natives and Europeans. In this portion of his duties he was greatly assisted by his wife, whom Sir Charles Metcalfe described as 'a most engaging woman,' and whose charities were famous during her stay in India, and much missed after her departure. The best description of her character and virtues is that given by Mr. Greville after her death in May, 1843. It should be read for the light it throws on the character of one who was most nearly associated with Lord William Bentinck in his public career of forty years, but about whom the records of Government are unavoidably silent.

CHAPTER VIII

EDUCATION

Of all the acts associated with the administration of Lord William Bentinck there was none more important or of greater consequence than the new education policy inaugurated in 1834, which was based on the establishment of English as the official language of the country. This policy was an innovation, and was regarded by some of the most experienced men in India as full of danger. The East India Company respected the language as well as the religion and customs of the people, and the Orientalist school predicted innumerable evils and misfortunes from any attempt to interfere with it. To introduce English into the schools and to make it the vehicle of knowledge was represented as destructive of the national learning, and to substitute the tongue of the European conqueror for Persian in the courts of law as certain to be followed by unpopularity, if not absolute animosity. In support of these views were to be found such venerable names as the Prinseps; but they were too far-fetched to carry the weight to which those who held them were entitled by their linguistic attainments and sympathy with the natives of India. The English school, as it was termed, was composed of younger men, and represented the more practical side of Indian administration. The late Sir Charles Trevelyan and Mr. Russell Colvin, who was Governor of the North-West Provinces in the first days of the Mutiny, were its principal leading men Sir Charles Metcalfe and others of the leaders, and of the day supported them.

It may be doubted how the contest would have resulted between these two opposing parties but for the efforts and genius of Macaulay. The Charter Act of 1833 provided for the appointment of an additional or Law-member to the Council of the Governor-General, and the post was offered to Mr. Macaulay, who had shown himself the ablest supporter of the India Bill in the House of Commons. He arrived in India before the end of the year, and he at once took a controlling part in the discussion of all matters relating to education and legal reform. It happened that at the moment of his arrival the subject of education was a burning topic on account of the difference of opinion prevailing in the General Committee of Public Instruction. The question in dispute was as to the principles on which the Government subsidies should be allotted to the different colleges that had been established by English initiative since Warren Hastings founded the first of them—the Calcutta College—in the year 1781. The main principle at stake was the question of the language in which instruction should be given, and the difference between the opposing parties has been summed up thus:—

'Half of the Committee called the "Orientalists" were for the continuation of the old system of stipends tenable for twelve or fifteen years, to students of Arabic and Sanskrit, and for liberal expenditure on the publication of works in these languages. The other half, called the "Anglicists," desired to reduce the expenditure on stipends held by "lazy and stupid schoolboys of 30 and 35 years of age," and to cut down the sums lavished on Sanskrit and Arabic printing. At this juncture, Government requested the Committee to prepare a scheme of instruction for a college at Agra. The Committee were utterly unable to agree on any plan. Five members were in favour of Arabic, Persian, and Sanskrit learning, and five in favour of English and the vernacular, with just so much of the Oriental learned languages as would be necessary to satisfy local prejudices.'

Macaulay on arriving in India was appointed President of this Committee, but he refused to act as such until the Governor-General had decided upon the language of instruction. In his capacity of Legislative member of Council, however, he was neither diffident nor inactive, and when the question was brought before Council by the rival parties, who addressed their arguments in the form of letters, dated 21st and 22nd January, 1835, respectively, he expressed his views on the matter in dispute in a masterly minute, dated 2nd February of that year, and from which we must quote the following paragraphs, as it is impossible to describe the points in dispute in clearer or more expressive language:—

'It does not appear to me that the Act of Parliament can by any art of construction be made to bear the meaning which has been assigned to it. It contains nothing about the particular languages or sciences which are to be studied. . . . . It is argued, or rather taken for granted, that by literature the Parliament can have meant only Arabic and Sanscrit literature, that they never would have given the honourable appellation of "a learned native" to a native who was familiar with the poetry of Milton, the metaphysics of Locke, and the physics of Newton; but that they meant to designate by that name only such persons as might have studied in the sacred books of the Hindus all the uses of kusa-grass and all the mysteries of absorption into the Deity. This does not appear to be a very satisfactory interpretation. To take a parallel case; suppose that the Pasha of Egypt, a country once superior in knowledge to the nations of Europe but now sunk far below them, were to appropriate a sum for the purpose of "reviving and promoting literature and encouraging learned natives of Egypt," would anybody infer that he meant the youth of his Pashalic to give years to the study of hieroglyphics, to search into all the doctrines disguised under the fable of Osiris, and to ascertain with all possible accuracy the ritual with which cats and onions were anciently adored? Would he be justly charged with inconsistency, if instead of employing his young subjects in deciphering obelisks he were to order them to be instructed in the English and French languages, and in all the sciences to which those languages are the chief keys? . . .

'The admirers of the Oriental system of education have used another argument which, if we admit it to be valid, is decisive against all change. They conceive that the public faith is pledged to the present system, and that to alter the appropriation of any of the funds which have hitherto been spent in encouraging the study of Arabic and Sanskrit would be downright spoliation. It is not easy to understand by what process of reasoning they can have arrived at this conclusion. The grants which are made from the public purse for the encouragement of literature differ in no respect from the grants which are made from the same purse for other objects of real or supposed utility. We found a sanatorium on a spot which we suppose to be healthy. Do we thereby pledge ourselves to keep a sanatorium there if the result should not answer our expectations? We commence the erection of a pier. Is it a violation of the public faith to stop the works if we afterwards see reason to believe that the building will be useless? The rights of property are undoubtedly sacred. But nothing endangers those rights so much as the practice now unhappily too common of attributing them to things to which they do not belong. . . .

'All parties seem to be agreed on one point, that the dialects commonly spoken among the natives of this part of India contain neither literary nor scientific information, and are moreover so poor and rude that until they are enriched from some other quarter it will not be easy to translate any valuable work into them. It seems to be admitted on all sides that the intellectual improvement of those classes of the people who have the means of pursuing higher studies can at present be effected only by means of some language not vernacular amongst them. What then shall that language be? One half of the Committee maintain that it should be the English. The other half strongly recommend the Arabic and Sanskrit. The whole question seems to me to be which language is the best worth knowing? I have no knowledge of either Sanscrit or Arabic. But I have done what I could to form a correct estimate of their value. I have read translations of the most celebrated Arabic and Sanskrit works. I have conversed both here and at home with men distinguished by their proficiency in the Eastern tongues. I am quite ready to take the Oriental learning at the valuation of the Orientalists themselves. I have never found one among them who could deny that a single shelf of a good European library was worth the whole native literature of India and Arabia. The intrinsic superiority of the Western literature is indeed fully admitted by those members of the Committee who support the Oriental plan of education. It will hardly be disputed, I suppose, that the department of literature in which the Eastern writers stand highest is poetry. And I certainly never met with any Orientalist who ventured to maintain that the Arabic and Sanskrit poetry could be compared to that of the great European nations. But when we pass from works of imagination to works in which facts are recorded and general principles investigated the superiority of the Europeans becomes absolutely immeasurable. It is, I believe, no exaggeration to say that all the historical information which has been collected from all the books written in the Sanskrit language is less valuable than what may be found in the most paltry abridgments used at preparatory schools in England. In every branch of physical or moral philosophy the relative position of the two nations is nearly the same.

'How then stands the case? We have to educate a people who cannot at present be educated by means of their mother tongue. We must teach them some foreign language. The claims of our own language it is hardly necessary to recapitulate. It stands pre-eminent even among the languages of the West. It abounds with works of imagination not inferior to the noblest which Greece has bequeathed to us; with models of every species of eloquence; with historical compositions which considered merely as narratives have seldom been surpassed, and which considered as vehicles of ethical and political instruction have never been equalled; with just and lively representations of human life and human nature; with the most profound speculation on metaphysics, morals, government, jurisprudence, and trade; with full and correct information respecting every experimental science which tends to preserve the health, to increase the comfort, or to expand the intellect of man. Whoever knows that language has ready access to all the vast intellectual wealth which all the wisest nations of the earth have created and hoarded in the course of ninety generations. It may safely be said that the literature now extant in that language is of far greater value than all the literature which 300 years ago was extant in all the languages of the world together. Nor is this all. In India, English is the language spoken by the ruling class. It is spoken by the higher class of natives at the seats of Government. It is likely to become the language of commerce throughout the seas of the East. It is the language of two great European communities which are rising, the one in the south of Africa, the other in Australasia; communities which are every year becoming more important and more closely connected with our Indian Empire. Whether we look at the intrinsic value of our literature or at the particular situation of this country we shall see the strongest reason to think that of all foreign tongues the English tongue is that which would be the most useful to our native subjects.

'The question now before us is simply whether, when it is in our power to teach this language, we shall teach languages in which by universal confession there are no books on any subject which deserve to be compared to our own; whether, when we can teach European science, we shall teach systems which by universal confession whenever they differ from those of Europe differ for the worse; and whether, when we can patronise sound philosophy and true history, we shall countenance at the public expense medical doctrines which would disgrace an English farrier, astronomy which would move laughter in girls at an English boarding-school, history abounding with kings thirty feet high and reigns 30,000 years long, and geography made up of seas of treacle and seas of butter. . . . The languages of

Western Europe civilised Russia. I cannot doubt that they will do for the Hindu what they have done for the Tartar. . . .

'The fact that the Hindu law is to be learned chiefly from Sanskrit books and the Muhammadan law from Arabic books has been much insisted on, but seems not to bear at all on the question. We are commanded by Parliament to ascertain and digest the laws of India. The assistance of a Law Commission has been given to us for that purpose. As soon as the code is promulgated the Shasters and the Hedaya will be useless to a Múnsif or Sadr Amín. I hope and trust that before the boys who are now entering at the Madrasa and the Sanskrit College have completed their studies this great work will be finished. It would be manifestly absurd to educate the rising generation with a view to a state of things which we mean to alter before they reach manhood.

'But there is yet another argument which seems even more untenable. It is said that the Sanskrit and Arabic are the languages in which the sacred books of a hundred millions of people are written, and that they are on that account entitled to peculiar encouragement. Assuredly it is the duty of the British Government in India to be not only tolerant but neutral on all religious questions. But to encourage the study of a literature admitted to be of small intrinsic value, only because that literature inculcates the most serious errors on the most important subjects, is a course hardly reconcilable with reason, with morality, or even with that very neutrality which ought, as we all agree, to be sacredly pursued. It is confessed that a language is barren of useful knowledge. We are to teach it because it is fruitful of monstrous superstitions. We are to teach false history, false astronomy, false medicine, because we find them in company with a false religion. We abstain, and I trust shall always abstain, from giving any public encouragement to those who are engaged in the work of converting natives to Christianity. And while we act thus can we reasonably and decently bribe men out of the revenues of the state to waste their youth in learning how they are to purify themselves after touching an ass, or what text of the Vedas they are to repeat to expiate the crime of killing a goat? . . .

'To sum up what I have said. I think it clear that we are not fettered by any pledge expressed or implied; that we are free to employ our funds as we choose; that we ought to employ them in teaching what is best worth knowing; that English is better worth knowing than Sanskrit or Arabic; that the natives are desirous to be taught English, and are not desirous to be taught Sanskrit or Arabic; that neither as the languages of law nor as the languages of religion have the Sanskrit and Arabic any peculiar claim to our encouragement; that it is possible to make natives of this country thoroughly good English scholars, and that to this end our efforts ought to be directed.'

The arguments recorded in this masterly Minute are unanswerable, and leave little or nothing further to be said on the subject of making the English language the vehicle of instruction in India, but the deliberate opinion of a practical Anglo-Indian administrator like Sir Charles Metcalfe must increase the weight attaching to the logic and acumen displayed in Macaulay's exposition of the question. And Metcalfe wrote the following plain words on the subject:—'The English language seems to me to be the channel through which we are most likely to convey improvement to the natives of India.'

Before Macaulay arrived in India, Lord William Bentinck had shown that his sympathies were in favour of English education. Among other acts pointing to this conclusion may be cited his invitation to Krishen Rao, head master of the school at Ságar, to visit Calcutta at his own personal expense, so that he might become better acquainted with European ways and civilisation. In such visits and personal contact he saw the best means of opening the minds of natives to the benefits of education. Full expression was given to these views in the celebrated Resolution of March 7, 1835, which finally decreed that English should be the official language of India.

The Orientalists prided themselves on being the better friends of the Indians, and they considered that the blow dealt to their classical languages would cramp the political future and injure the interests of the natives. Experience has refuted these opinions, if indeed they were ever tenable. There can be no doubt that the students of Sanskrit and Arabic would never have been admitted to the same share with ourselves in the government of India that they now possess as fluent masters of the English language. The Orientalists were in reality the enemies of the Hindu race, and the English reformers, headed by Lord William Bentinck, Macaulay, and Metcalfe, its true friends. The latter were right not only in principle, but in anticipating that the natives would master our language with ease, and become as fluent in it as the subject Gauls and Africans became in the Imperial language of Rome. Even if the result had furnished a less complete vindication of their views it would still have been impossible to arraign their policy, for it was the only one capable of satisfying the requirements of an alien domination such as we had established in India, and at the same time of providing the inhabitants with a legitimate share in the government of their country. There must of necessity be some bond of union between the ruling power and the subject if the relationship is to prove enduring, and in India it is out of the question to expect that either race or religion will supply the desired link. There was left only language, and it cannot be doubted that if English had not been placed in a superior position to every other language spoken in India there would have remained a wide and unbridged abyss between the rulers and the ruled. The educated native of India, whether he be Hindu or Muhammadan, now speaks English with as much fluency as can be expected in the use of a foreign tongue, and there is no doubt that to this cause is mainly due the growing conviction in India that the interests of the two countries are identical. That native opinion has taken this desirable course is largely if not exclusively attributable to the resolution adopted by Lord William Bentinck in March, 1835, to make English the official language of India for admission into the public service and for the dispensation of justice in its higher forms.

The mention of admission into the public service suggests the consideration of the most important consequence of that resolution. From the evidence produced before the Select Committee in 1853, on the occasion of the final renewal of the East India Company's Charter, it appeared that the clause in the Act of 1833 relating to the admission of natives to higher appointments was inserted at the instance of Lord William Bentinck, who never ceased to recommend its adoption, and with this positive statement before us it will be readily understood how determined Lord William Bentinck was to make English the basis of education in India. If the education resolution had not been carried into effect the clause in the Charter Act on the subject of the employment of natives would have been a dead letter, and it would have been impossible for Sir Charles Trevelyan to have placed on record in his evidence before the Select Committee of 1853 this important opinion :—

> 'To Lord William Bentinck belongs the great praise of having placed our dominion in India on its proper foundation in the recognition of the great principle that India is to be governed for the benefit of the Indians, and that the advantages which we derive from it should only be such as are incidental to, and inferential from, that course of proceeding.'

If English had not been adopted there would have been no possibility of the admission of natives of India to the higher branches of the service, in which they have since shown conspicuous ability, and reduced the cost of government. The advocacy of the only possible common language formed part of the policy of education and enlightenment which is rightly associated with the name of Lord William

Bentinck, and was the consummating act of his promotion of a knowledge of English literature and science, as well as of the English tongue, among the educated classes of India. As the result it was said that 'the scale of estimation in which natives were held by Europeans was advanced by Lord William Bentinck.' This improvement was rendered the more apparent by the marked decline in the consideration in which natives were held that followed the departure of Lord William Bentinck—a decline which showed the inevitable reaction among the official classes, who had not regarded the Governor-General's policy with favour, and who were naturally disinclined to treat on any terms of equality the then uneducated Bengalis. The work of placing the social relations of the two races on a permanently satisfactory basis must be a matter of time, and it is only necessary to state that Lord William Bentinck laid the foundation for a better condition of things.

The question of the Press is intimately connected with that of education. Sir John Kaye states that 'the Press had been practically free for the whole period of the administration of Lord William Bentinck,' but his departure left the crowning act in the emancipation of the Press for his devoted lieutenant and temporary successor, Sir Charles, afterwards Lord, Metcalfe. This was effected in June, 1835, by the repeal of the Press Regulations of 1823. Lord William's Press policy had been, with one exception, marked by great liberality and by a breadth of view which was not too common in the England of his day. His true sentiments seem to have been expressed when he said that 'he knew of no subject which the Press might not fairly discuss.' The somewhat different line that he took in connexion with the Batta case, when the final orders of the Court were given, was to be explained by the special circumstances of the time. The feelings of the military officers of the Company were very excited at the proposed reduction of their most cherished perquisite, and it was absolutely necessary after a very free discussion of the question during several years to peremptorily close it, when it had been decided beyond possibility of dispute that Batta should be reduced. It was in special relation to this matter and not as a general principle that Lord William Bentinck wrote the sentence which has furnished his enemies with a charge of inconsistency, that 'it is necessary in my opinion for the public safety that the Press in India should be kept under the most rigid control.' With regard even to the question as to whether officials should be allowed to contribute to the newspapers he was disposed to take a lenient view and to give them considerable latitude, always provided that they did not make use of official information to criticise the acts of their immediate superiors.

In the three great questions which were really dependent on the selection of English as the language to be used by the Government and its agents, Lord William Bentinck took a prominent and active part on the side of native progress. Those questions were the admission of natives to the higher grades of the public service, the dissemination of modern culture among the upper classes of the natives with a view to their admission on terms of friendship into European society, and, thirdly, the emancipation of the Press for the purpose of creating and strengthening a healthy public opinion. It is impossible to measure the magnitude of the service conferred on the Indian peoples by Lord William Bentinck in all these matters. The most severe criticism that can be levelled at his proceedings is not that he was wrong in his policy, or that the principles upon which it was based were untenable, but that he was putting them in practice somewhat before the time was ripe. The financial position of the Indian Government, with its annual deficit and growing responsibilities, forbade the postponement of the admission of natives of India into the public service. It was absolutely indispensable to employ the only men who could work for a reasonable payment, and who moreover possessed a perfect knowledge of the character and customs of the governed. A persistence in keeping the administration of India as an exclusive monopoly for the nominees of the East India Company would have ended in bankruptcy. In the major part of his reform Lord William Bentinck therefore did not act too soon. He opened the gates of the public service partly because he saw that it was a mistaken and impossible policy to exclude the natives of India from a fuller share in the government of the country, and partly because it was necessary to reduce the expenses of government. Both English and native interests were benefited in the long run, and the service to his own country was not less real though less apparent than that rendered to the natives of India. This policy explains and justifies the passage with which Macaulay closes his brilliant essay on Lord Clive when he speaks of 'the veneration with which the latest generation of Hindus will contemplate the statue of Lord William Bentinck.'

CHAPTER IX

EXTERNAL AFFAIRS

ALTHOUGH the Governor-Generalship of Lord William Bentinck was essentially peaceful, and its main interest centred in domestic and administrative reforms, it must not be supposed that external affairs presented no features of importance, or that during his tenure of power the foreign policy of India became practically a dead letter. If there was no foreign war, and if tranquillity was maintained on the frontiers, there were still negotiations that exercised a considerable influence on the policy of India and her neighbours in future years, and during the whole of his stay in the country the course of events west of the Indus was carefully watched, and what the best policy would be in certain eventualities formed a subject of constant discussion in official circles. It may seem strange, but it is none the less a fact, that Anglo-Indians were then divided into schools of forward and stationary policies quite as much as now, and that the possibility of a Russian invasion of India was discussed as freely as it has been since. While some ardent spirits advocated the annexation of the Punjab and Sind, and wished to have commercial agents at Kábul, Herát, and even Bokhara, others deprecated any advance beyond the Sutlej, and would have left the custody of the Indus (which Akbar called the ditch of Delhi) to the Sikhs. The important Minute with which this chapter is closed shows that Lord William Bentinck was deeply interested in all these questions, and that he had a definite opinion as to how they should be treated.

The most important branch of the foreign policy of the Government of India in Lord William Bentinck's time was unquestionably the relations to be maintained with Ranjít Singh, the powerful ruler of the Sikhs. Those relations had subsisted for more than twenty years when he assumed charge of the government, but the increasing interest in Afghánistán, owing to the prolonged uncertainty as to whether the sovereign power in that state would finally fall to Dost Muhammad or Shuja ul Mulk, rendered them of special interest during the last three years of Lord William's stay in India. In 1805 Ranjít Singh was merely one of the chiefs of the Punjab, but three years later he had become generally known as the Mahárájá. When the Indian Government, alarmed by Napoleon's schemes in Persia for the invasion of India, sent in 1808 envoys to Kábul and Teherán, it also resolved to depute an officer to the camp of Ranjít Singh with the view of negotiating a defensive alliance and concerting measures for the protection of the Punjab and British India. Mr. Metcalfe, then a young man, was entrusted with this mission, and executed it with exceptional tact and ability. But, strange to say, Ranjít Singh, of all the potentates we approached, was the only one indisposed to play a friendly part.

Our agent declared that 'our propositions were met by the most striking display of jealousy, distrust, and suspicion,' and that Ranjít Singh thought only of turning the presence of the British mission in his camp to advantage for his own personal ends. His main object was to incorporate in his dominion the Sikh states lying between the Sutlej and the Jumna, but as soon as the Indian Government realised his intentions it forbade his intervention in that quarter by taking the states of Patiála and its neighbours under its own special protection. Although Ranjít Singh resorted to every device within the scope of diplomacy to attain his object, he yielded with a good grace when he found that we were in earnest, and that he could only carry out his policy by appealing to a force which he did not possess. For twenty years after the mission referred to Ranjít Singh preserved a friendly, if vigilant, policy towards us, and if Mr. Metcalfe failed in the immediate object of his mission, he was so far successful that he provided the basis of a more cordial understanding.

Immediately after the arrival of Lord William Bentinck one of those frontier disputes which cannot be avoided between neighbouring states arose in connexion with Wadwan, but its satisfactory arrangement showed that the Punjab ruler knew how to gracefully retreat when he could not carry his point. This incident sinks into insignificance beside the more important matters that arose out of the attempts of the Duráni exile, Sháh Shuja ul Mulk, to recover the Afghán throne by the aid of Ranjít Singh and the British Government. In June, 1829, he wrote acquainting the Indian Government with his proposed alliance with Ranjít Singh for the recovery of Kábul, and it so happened that the receipt of this letter coincided with instructions from home to acquire the control of trade on the river Indus. Although we did not then comply with his request, he was not discouraged from his undertaking by the British Government, which provided for him and his family a liberal pension. The first step taken by Lord William Bentinck towards carrying out his instructions was to commence negotiations with the Amirs of Sind for opening the Indus to Indian commerce. The negotiations took some time, but at last a treaty was signed in April, 1832, and a subsequent convention was concluded in December, 1834. At the same time that it negotiated with the power which held the approach to the Indus from the sea, the Indian Government made friendly overtures to Ranjít Singh, whose attitude had become more conciliatory to us. A special mission under the charge of Alexander Burnes, who was entrusted with a letter from William IV and a present of English horses to the Mahárájá, was sent to Lahore in July, 1831, and in the following October Lord William Bentinck had a personal interview with Ranjít Singh at Rúpar on the Sutlej. This meeting was of a strictly ceremonious character—the Mahárájá being accompanied by 16,000 picked troops, and the Governor-General's escort consisting of a chosen force of English and native regiments.

The commercial treaty was not signed by Ránjít Singh until December, 1832, but that the Rúpar interview was not devoid of political importance was shown by the increased and more open support extended by the Sikh Mahárájá to the projects of Shuja ul Mulk after its occurrence. It is very unlikely that this astute ruler would have shown his hand so freely if he had not felt sure of our acquiescence and moral support. The result of Lord William Bentinck's diplomacy with the Lion of the Punjab was a great increase in Ranjít's friendliness to us, and the establishment of that understanding which resulted in the alliance a few years later against Afghánistán, and which held good through all the troubles at Kábul ten years afterwards. There is no necessity here to challenge or uphold the wisdom of that policy. It is enough to record Lord William Bentinck's marked success in coming to a satisfactory understanding with Ranjít Singh, who at an earlier period of his career had been hostile and even defiant.

But something must be briefly said on the subject

of Sháh Shuja's first attempt with Indian resources to reconquer Afghanistan. Equipped with a considerable sum of money by Ranjít Singh, he left Ludhiána at the head of a few hundred men. By the time he reached Shikárpur on the Indus his following had swelled to an army 30,000 strong, but there had also commenced the misfortunes of this ill-starred expedition.

The Amirs of Sind, imitating the example of Ranjít Singh, had promised him supplies and money, but alarmed at the largeness of the Afghán force they requested Sháh Shuja to hasten his departure from their territory. This did not suit his plans or convenience, and the allies of one day became the bitter opponents of the next. They even resorted to arms, and in a sanguinary battle fought at Rori on the Indus, in January, 1834, the Sind forces suffered a complete overthrow. This battle settled the difficulty, for the Amirs paid up all, and more than all, they had promised, and Sháh Shuja hastened on to Kandahár. The condition of Afghánistán then was as a house divided against itself. There was no central authority and no single chief. The able Dost Muhammad ruled in Kábul, and his brothers held possession of the different provinces. But there was no union even against Shuja ul Mulk, and when Dost Muhammad's request for an alliance (made to the English Government in May, 1833) was rejected, it looked as if the Bárakzáis could not make any head against Sháh Shuja, and the first events of the campaign bore out this assumption. The Kandahár forces were overthrown, and close siege was laid to the town, which was on the eve of surrendering when Dost Muhammad arrived at the head of a relieving army. A pitched battle was fought near Kaṇdahár, and the result hung for some time in the balance. Had the whole army fought with the intrepidity of two Hindustáni regiments led by an English officer named Campbell the result must have been favourable to Sháh Shuja, but his Afghán followers had, even in the short space that had elapsed since they left Ludhiána, been alienated by his faults, and they deserted him in the crisis of the battle. His own rashness and want of courage seem to have contributed to his overthrow. He fled the field on the dispersion of his forces, and after several adventures in Balúchistán and Sind he succeeded in regaining the safety of his old refuge at Ludhiána. The main objects of Lord William Bentinck's policy in this quarter were to convert the Indus into the ditch of British India, to associate the Sikhs and the Sind valley with us in its defence, and to create a friendly Afghánistán as a buffer-state between India and any possible invader.

Lord William Bentinck's attention was directed to the East as well as the West. He was specially interested in the future of Singapur, a position of commanding importance which we owe to the genius of Sir Stamford Raffles, who acquired what might become the Gibraltar of Asia by purchase in 1819. Strangely enough its importance was not realised until a comparatively recent period, and in April,

1830, and again in September, 1833, we find Lord William Bentinck inviting schemes to increase the population of both Singapur and Penang. In 1832 he transferred the capital of the Straits Settlements from Prince of Wales Island to Singapur. The introduction of steam and the growth of trade between India and Australasia have altered all this, and the future prosperity of Singapur may now be deemed assured, but Lord William Bentinck is entitled to all the credit of having realised this when most people were sceptical as to the value of the position.

There was another matter not immediately connected with any place or country, but bearing generally on the external relations of India, in which Lord William Bentinck took a lively concern, and that was the establishment of steam communication between India and England. He encouraged every scheme calculated to promote this object, and it was largely due to his initiation and efforts that success was attained at such an early stage of the question. The receipt of news from Europe by some more rapid conveyance than a sailing ship had long been an object of prime importance with the East India Company, and during the wars with France many schemes had been tried for this purpose. The agents of the Company and the British Consuls at Bussora, Aleppo, and in Egypt were actively employed in the transmission of despatches to India, sometimes by the Euphrates and the Persian Gulf, and sometimes by the Red Sea. Before Lord William Bentinck reached India the first experiment had also been made in steam navigation between the two countries. A small vessel named 'The Enterprise' sailed in 1825 from England to India, partly by steam and partly by sailing, in less than four months; but as considerable disappointment was felt at the time taken, no further experiment was attempted for a few years.

In the meantime another question demanded a prompt answer—as to the rival claims of the Cape and overland routes. Between the merits of these routes Lord William Bentinck was called upon to decide, and in August, 1830, he gave his unqualified decision in favour of the Red Sea route over that by the Cape for the despatch of letters and news. He was, no doubt, induced to form this conclusion by the successful journey of the 'Hugh Lindsay' steamer, which steamed from Bombay to Suez in one month—a time that was subsequently reduced to twenty-two days. The Indian Government then hastened to purchase the necessary steamers to keep up communications by this route, and Mr. Waghorn, who had strenuously advocated its advantages, and whose name is generally associated with the origin of this route, was rewarded with the command of one of them. Lord William Bentinck returned to the subject in a minute dated 12 June, 1832, on the question of establishing steam communication between Egypt and England in connexion with that already in progress by the Red Sea from Egypt to India. But his opinion on the subject was given in its most interesting form before a Select Committee of the House of Commons in 1837. He said:—

'It is through the means of a quite safe and frequent communication between all India and England that the natives of India in person will be enabled to bring their complaints and grievances before the authorities and the country; that large numbers of disinterested travellers will have it in their power to report to their country at home the nature and circumstances of this distant portion of the Empire. This result I hope will be to rouse the shameful apathy and indifference of Great Britain to the concerns of India; and by thus bringing the eye of the British public to bear upon India it may be hoped that the desired amelioration may be accomplished.'

Reference has been made in the earlier paragraphs of this chapter to the motives which led to the treaties with Ranjít Singh and the Amirs of Sind, and to the encouragement of the Afghán exile, Shuja ul Mulk. It was in Lord William Bentinck's time that the possibility of a Russian invasion of India was fairly faced and discussed, and his parting legacy to the Government of India was a masterly minute in which he reviewed the military position of the country and considered the question of an attack by a Russian army associated with an irregular force of Central Asian and Afghán adventurers. As we had only gained India after a struggle with our old European rivals, the French, it was natural for us to contemplate the possibility of another European invasion of India, and during the earlier years of this century the ambitious schemes of Napoleon kept us constantly on the alert. In 1830 fear of France in India at all events had disappeared, but in its place had arisen a keen and not ill-founded apprehension that Russia might prove a more formidable and persistent adversary. This sentiment led to two inquiries: first, what was the strength of the position we held in India; and secondly, what were our resources for meeting an invader; and they are exhaustively considered in the minute already referred to. But before quoting Lord William Bentinck's opinion some evidence of the prevalent feeling among Anglo-Indian officials may be given, and this cannot be furnished in a better form or with greater authority than by using the words of Sir Charles Metcalfe:—

'Some say that our Empire in India rests on opinion, others on main force. It in fact depends on both. We could not keep the country by opinion if we had not a considerable force, and no force that we could pay would be sufficient if it were not aided by the opinion of our invincibility. Our force does not operate so much by its actual strength as by the impression which it produces, and that impression is the opinion by which we hold India.'

Commenting on Lord William Bentinck's minute Sir Charles wrote:—

'He admits that we have no hold on the affections of our subjects; that our native army is taken from a disaffected population; that our European soldiery are too few to be of much avail against any extensive plan of insurrection. This is quite enough and more than I have hitherto alluded to, for it is impossible to contemplate the possibility of disaffection in our army without seeing at once the full force of our danger. As long as our native army is faithful, and we can pay enough for it, we can keep India in order by its instrumentality, but if the instrument should turn against us where would be the British power? Echo answers, where? It is impossible to support a sufficient army of Europeans to take the place of our native army. The late Governor-General appears also to adopt in some measure the just remark of Sir John Malcolm that 'in an Empire like that of India we are always in danger, and it is impossible to conjecture the form in which it may approach.' This sentiment expresses the reality of the case in perhaps the truest manner.'

On another occasion, speaking of 'the instability of our Indian Empire,' he said, 'we were sitting on a barrel of gunpowder in India which might explode at any moment.' With regard to a possible Russian invasion Sir Charles was in favour of waiting on events, and keeping the military expenditure strictly within the limits of our financial resources. He was in favour of every increase being made in the European garrison of India that could be borne by the revenues of that country, and of deferring exceptional measures until the danger had become more tangible and nearer. What is surprising is that with this clear perception in the highest quarters of the insecurity of our position in India in 1835, there should have been such rash over-confidence in 1857, when it was relatively weaker, and 'the native army taken from a disaffected population' constituted more than ever the basis of our power.

Sixty years ago the possibility of a Russian invasion of India was exceedingly remote, and so many difficulties remained to be overcome, and such was the extent of the intervening distance, that ordinary men might be excused for deeming such a project chimerical. Yet practical and far-seeing statesmen like Lord William Bentinck and Sir Charles Metcalfe not merely discussed the extent and probable date of the arrival of the danger, but laid down the best mode of dealing with it. Sir Charles Metcalfe, who was opposed to even commercial missions to Kábul, and who was the first to prominently advocate the doctrines of 'masterly inactivity,' was content to leave the result to the natural course of events—being of opinion that the Indian garrison could render a good account of any Russian force likely to reach the frontier. On the other hand, Lord William Bentinck, whose policy was of a more vigorous description, drew up the following minute on the whole aspect of our position in India, and although the facts are altered and events have produced many changes, its value is still very considerable, and its historical interest is quite unimpeachable.

Minute by the Governor-General and Commander-in-Chief, March 13th, 1835.

Before I proceed to describe what the constitution of the army is, and to offer an opinion as to what it ought to be, a preliminary enquiry seems to be necessary as to the specific dangers by which our dominion may be assailed. It is easy enough to determine upon the general principles to be followed and the great end to be attained, viz. that the military body should be so constituted and regulated that by its imposing moral attitude, by its established fidelity and allegiance, it should render hopeless all internal rebellion, as also that by the adequacy of its numbers and by its reputation for discipline and valour, it should be able, as well in the general opinion as in the reality, to overcome any foreign attack. But the elements both of our danger and of our security are of more difficult estimation, and without an exact knowledge both of the one and the other, it is very possible that the precautions adopted for our security may become the very means of our subversion.

Of internal dangers nobody, I believe, entertains less alarm than myself. In answer to those almost universal representations from authorities of the existence of danger, and of the consequent necessity of maintaining a large native army, I have in vain asked to have pointed out to me what the danger is—where are the Horse, Foot, and Artillery by which we are to be ejected? The most recent document of this kind that I have seen is the minute of the Commander-in-Chief at Madras, who describes disaffection as everywhere prevailing, and argues in consequence against any reduction of the army, and thinks necessary an augmentation of it. Indeed, there are those who contend for the same establishment now as when Haidar and Tipú were in the plenitude of their power, and when several substantive states existed in other parts of India. But in Madras, as in Bengal, there no longer exists a single chief, or a combination of chiefs, who possess even the semblance of a military force. Nor are there any large masses of the population who have the least disposition to rebel against our authority. A vague expression is often used that ours is a Government of opinion. Our security rests upon a very much better foundation, upon the fact which every one from his own observation and experience is thoroughly convinced of, and which is true, that our power is irresistible.

But though no danger appears in any real or tangible shape, it must be allowed when one hundred millions of people are under the control of a Government which has no hold whatever on their affections, when out of this population is formed that army upon the fidelity of which we rely principally for our preservation, when our European troops, of whose support under all circumstances we are alone sure, are so exceedingly limited in number and efficiency as to be of little avail against any extensive plan of insurrection, then indeed the truth of that expression of Sir John Malcolm is not without force, that in an Empire like India we are always in danger, and it is impossible to conjecture the form in which it may approach. This state of uncertainty is greatly aggravated by our conditions of peace, by the spread of knowledge, and by the operations of the press—all of which are tending rapidly as well to weaken the respect entertained for the European character and the prestige of British superiority as to elevate the native character, to make these men alive to their own rights and more sensible of their power. Of the dangers of our old position, upon which men's minds continue to harp and against which they see no security but the largest possible native army, I have no apprehension.

But there is much more reason to fear the changes incidental to our new position of peace and more enlightened state of mind,—a higher elevation of character, knowledge, improved morality, courage, all concurring causes that must produce effects to be dealt with by a very different philosophy from that which has hitherto obtained. So much for internal evils.

I shall now consider the danger from without, thinking of this as of the other, that there is no ground for any present alarm, but that we do not know the time or the quarter, when and where it may appear, but thinking in like

M 2

manner of both, that it is by immediate preparation only that security can be obtained, and that relief will be too late if we wait, as would be most convenient, the actual occurrence of the mischief.

The following is a brief abstract of our military position. British India may be assailed from the north by the Gúrkhas; from the east by the Burmese; from the north-west by the Sikhs, the Afgháns, and the hordes of Central Asia, in co-operation or otherwise with Persia and Russia; from the sea on all the other sides of her territory.

An attack from the Gúrkhas might partially succeed as a diversion against our hill provinces, but without cavalry or artillery their efforts on the plains could only terminate in disgrace and defeat.

The Burmese have proved themselves totally unequal to compete with our forces in the field.

An attack from the sea, even supposing a momentary superiority against us on that element, could only produce an insulated debarkation, devoid of all the necessary requisites for taking the field or to subsist in a fixed position.

The only real danger with which we may be threatened must come from the north-west, and consequently to that important line of operation our main attention should be turned.

Under its present able and judicious leader it is not possible that the forces of the Punjab will be ever directed against us. Ranjít Singh is old and infirm, and there is no apparent probability that the wisdom of his rule will be inherited by his successor. Troubles, upon his decease, will certainly arise, and it is impossible to foresee the result as relates to the line of conduct which we may be called upon to pursue.

The present state of Afghánistán presents no cause of alarm to India. The success that attended the wretched army that Sháh Shuja had under his feeble guidance affords the best proof of the weakness of the Afghán power. The assumption of the supremacy by Dost Muhammad Khán may possibly give greater strength and consolidation to the general confederacy. It is much to be desired that this state should acquire sufficient stability to form an intermediate barrier between India and Persia.

Persia, in its distracted state since the death of the late King, is unequal to any great effort unassisted by Russia, but the co-operation of 20,000 Russians from the Arrus would speedily terminate the civil war, and the advance of the combined force would give them in the first campaign possession of Herát, the key of Kábul.

It is the interest of Russia to extend and strengthen the Persian Empire, which occupies a central position between the double lines of operation of the Autocrat to the eastward and to the westward, and as Persia can never be a rival of Russia the augmentation of her strength can only increase the offensive means of Russia.

From the days of Peter the Great to the present time the views of Russia have been turned to the obtaining possession of that part of Central Asia which is watered by the Oxus and joins the eastern shore of the Caspian. The latest accounts from Kábul state they are building a fort between the Caspian and Khiva. This is their best line of operation against India, but it can only be considered at present as a very distant speculation.

The line of operation of a Russo-Persian army to advance upon Herát is short and easy; the distances are as follows:—

From the Arrus to Tabriz	60 miles.
Tabriz to Teherán . . .	300
Teherán to Muschid . .	601
Muschid to Herát . . .	228
Total . . .	1189

In the campaigns against the Turks the army of Georgia

supplied Paskewitch with 30,000 men. It may therefore be assumed that the same army could assist Persia with an equal number as an auxiliary force. With a good understanding between the two Governments, with time for preparation, and with good management there could be no difficulty in transporting this force to Herát. The Russians are accustomed to move in countries similarly circumstanced. In Turkey the Russian army always carried with it two months' supply of grain and handmills for grinding it, but they never issue any part of this supply until all other means of obtaining it have failed.

What the policy of Russia might be after taking possession of Herát it is unnecessary now to consider, but it is impossible to deny that she might arrive at that point in legitimate support of her ally, the King of Persia, and it is equally difficult to deny that from that point she may proclaim a crusade against British India, in which she would be joined by all the warlike restless tribes that formed the overwhelming force of Timúr. The distances from Herát to Attock are:—

Herát to Kandahár	560 miles.
Kandahár to Ghazni	190
Ghazni to Kábul	82
Kábul to Attock	200
	1032

The Afghán confederacy, even if cordially united, would have no means to resist the power of Russia and Persia. They probably would make a virtue of necessity and join the common cause, receiving in reward for their co-operation the promise of all the possessions that had been wrested from them by Ranjít Singh, and expecting also to reap no poor harvest from the plunder of India. But however this may be, it will be sufficient to assume the possibility that a Russian force of 20,000 men fully equipped, accompanied with a body of 100,000 horse, may reach the shores of the Indus, that

Ranjít Singh has no means to resist their advance, and that the invaders, having crossed the Indus into the Punjab, would find themselves in possession of the parts of India, the most fertile of resources in every kind, and secure on every side from being harassed and attacked even if they had not on their side a body of irregular cavalry much more numerous and efficient than any we have to oppose to them.

I shall assume, then, that the attack against which we have to provide is to consist of the above-mentioned force. I shall now proceed to inquire into the composition of the army of India, of the physical and moral qualities of the native armies of the different Presidencies, and of the adequacy and efficiency of the present proportion of our European force to our security and defence against all dangers.

In the margin[1] is inserted an abstract of the rank and file of all descriptions in the native armies of the three Presidencies—their height and weight, and the countries from whence they are recruited.

It appears from the annexed statements that the whole of

[1] RANK AND FILE OF THE THREE ARMIES.

Regular Infantry.		*Irregulars.*	
		Infantry.	
Bengal, 74 regiments	50,320	Bengal, 10 regiments	7504
Madras, 52 „	35,360	Bombay, 1 „	680
Bombay, 26 „	17,680		8184
	103,360		
Regular Cavalry.		Cavalry.	
Bengal, 10 regiments	4440	Bengal, 4 regiments	2526
Madras, 8 „	3552	Bombay, 1 „	832
Bombay, 3 „	1332		
	9324		3358

Total Regular Native Troops	112,684
Total Irregulars	11,542

the Bengal army, and one-half of that of Bombay, including all the cavalry, are Hindustánis. The Madras army is recruited principally from their own territories, and has only a small portion of Bengal men in their ranks. When at Utakamand all the Governments were requested to submit to a Military Committee the following question, 'Whether the order of the Court of Directors, issued about three years ago, restricting the recruiting of each of the three armies to the limits of its own Presidency, had operated beneficially; or whether it would be better to permit the Madras and Bombay armies to recruit as formerly in the Bengal territory?' the question did not apply to the Bengal army. The Madras Committee recommend that in the cavalry no alteration should be made, the men being chiefly Mussulmans from the Karnátik. The number of Hindus in each regiment amount to about fifty, which it is proposed to increase to an hundred. In the infantry they think that a proportion of Bengal men, about an hundred per regiment, might be introduced with advantage. In the Golundauze one-fourth of the whole are from the Bengal Provinces.

The Bombay Committee report that the Court's restrictive order has been totally inoperative, because, though the order

---

Average of Heights and Weights.

	Height. ft.	Height. in.	Weight. st.	Weight. lbs.
Bengal Infantry.				
Recruited generally in the Upper Provinces of Bengal	5	7·82	9	0·8
Madras Infantry.				
Men formerly recruit boys	5	6·36	7	9 73
Madrassis recruited	5	6·34	8	1·10
Hindustanis recruited	5	6·59	8	5·28
Bombay Infantry.				
Men formerly recruit boys	5	4·75	8	5·15
Konkanis recruited	5	5·5	8	5·25
Deccanis ,,	5	5·5	8	9·25
Hindustanis ,,	5	6 3	9	0·5

had been so far obeyed that no recruiting parties had been sent to Bengal, yet the Bengal men having voluntarily presented themselves for enlistment, they had been engaged as before. The only change recommended by the Committee is that, for the purpose of getting a better description of men, recruiting parties shall, as before, be sent to Bengal[1].

One of the members, Major Robertson, dissents from his colleagues. He prefers recruiting exclusively from the Bombay territories, with the exception of the cavalry and Golundauze, 'who, requiring a much larger description of men, must have recourse to Hindustan.'

From the preceding statements it appears that the Hindustáni is larger and more robust than the native south of the Narbadá, and the presumption must be that he is considered a more powerful if not a better soldier. His habits, indeed, are much more military, for not only, as appears above, does he go to seek service in Bombay, but the infantry in the service of the Rájá of Nágpur, as well as the Nizam's contingent, consist entirely of Hindustánis. In a late letter from the Resident of Haidarábád he mentions that one of the Arabs, or of the Horsemen from our Bengal Province of Rohilkhand, was equal to ten or twenty of the other men of the Nizam's force; and in the attempt recently made by Sháh Shuja to recover his territories, it was the battalion of Hindustánis and the Rohillas, under an officer of the name of Campbell, that was particularly distinguished.

I have not read without surprise the pretensions set forth in behalf of the Madras army. Sir Thomas Munro upon

[1] The following statement would seem to support the opinion that the Hindustánis engaged at Bombay are inferior in stature and character to those of the Bengal army:—

Infantry.	Height. ft.	in.	Cavalry, all Hindustánis. Corporal Punishment.	
Bengal	5	$7\frac{82}{100}$	Bengal	$1\frac{4}{10}$ per cent.
Bombay	5	$6\frac{1}{2}$	Bombay	42

A more severe discipline is supposed to prevail in the Bombay army.

many occasions advocates their occupation of the whole of the Peninsula south of the Narbadá. I submit the following extracts from his correspondence (A.D. 1820):—

'The Narbadá is unquestionably the proper boundary between Bengal and Madras, not only on account of its natural barrier formed by the river and the broad range of hills which accompany it, but of its being the line of separation between the Deccan and Hindustán, and between natives speaking different languages. The Bengal army, composed of men from Hindustán, dislike serving south of the Narbadá, and do not readily assimilate either with the natives of the country or with the Madras troops.'

I must presume that the Bombay army was at that time upon a very low establishment, and had no Hindustánis in its ranks. The dislike of the natives of Hindustán to serve south of the Narbadá has subsequently been proved to be entirely unfounded. The Government and army of Bombay are quite disregarded. Again (A.D. 1820):—

'When Haidarábád and Nágpur were great foreign and independent states' (and more likely to act against us than with us) 'the immediate control of Bengal was right, more especially as it did not affect the authority of the Madras Government over its army, of which only two battalions were several years at Haidarábád, but both Haidarábád and Nágpur are as completely dependent upon us as Mysore. They must at some period or other fall entirely into our hands, and the internal administration must in the meantime be chiefly directed by our Resident. At present the discipline of our army is much injured by our having 20,000 men beyond our frontier removed in a great measure from our control[1].'

Again (A.D. 1804):—

'I am sorry to hear it reported that it had been in agitation to relieve the subsidiary force at Haidarábád with Bengal troops, I think there are many strong public grounds for having no Bengal troops either there or at Poona. It is easier to carry on war in all the countries south of the Narbadá from Mysore than from Bengal. Where troops are in all respects equal there is still an advantage in having those who are to act together drawn from one

[1] This will be in part obviated by the transfer of a General Officer from the ceded districts to Haidarábád.

and not from different establishments, but the local troops are perhaps in some respects superior to those of Bengal. They are more regular, more tractable, more patient under privations, and they have been more accustomed to military operations.'

These remarks are more applicable to 1804 than to 1835. There are no enemies to war against. The greater experience in military operations now rather belongs to the Bengal troops, and the preference assigned to the Madras sepoy for certain qualities would not now be as readily admitted.

I have quoted largely from Sir Thomas Munro because I consider his authority superior to all others, but allowance must be made in the present case for a spirit of partiality, if not of partizanship, which as a Madras officer it was natural for him to feel. But it is impossible for any dispassionate observer who has seen the Madras sepoys not to say that their physical defects and delicate frame, supposing all other qualities equal, render them very inferior to the Northern Hindustánis, and that consequently as a body of men they are inferior to either of the other armies. The regulated standard of each army is noted in the margin[1].

I come next to the Bombay army, composed in equal proportions of Hindustánis and of men from their own proper territories. It would have been satisfactory if the Committee, who do not recommend any change in this divided com-

[1] BENGAL.

M.C., 8 August, 1796, Carrol's code, chap. lx, sec. 42. No sepoy is to be entertained who is not 5 ft. 5 in. high, or who is under 16 or above 30 years of age, unless in the latter case he shall have served before.

MADRAS.

The standard of the Madras army was raised in 1829 from 5 ft. 4 in. to 5 ft. 6 in. for Horse Artillery and Cavalry, and to 5 ft. 5 in. for Infantry of the line. Before 1829 the standard for all appears to have been 5 ft. 4 in.

BOMBAY.

The lowest standard for the Cavalry is 5 ft. 6 in., age 24 yrs. For Infantry 5 ft 3 in., age not above 22 yrs. For Grenadiers 5 ft. 6 in. and upwards.

position, had stated their reasons for it. The Bombay men seem to have no advantage in strength and size over the Madras sepoy.

I have often had occasion to remark upon the expensive character of the Bombay establishment, urging always the expediency of a compulsory order for the adjustment of their expenditure to their income. And in no instance has this assertion such strong confirmation as in respect to the formation of the Military Establishment. The army of Bombay consists of:—

Native Infantry	17,680
„ Cavalry	1,322
	19,002

To superintend this small force they have one Lieutenant-General and three Major-Generals, the same general staff as in the other Presidencies, with all the appendages of commissariat, ordnance establishments, pay and audit departments, &c. belonging to a large army. I beg a reference to the general distribution abstract of the Bengal army furnished by the Quartermaster-General, in which it will appear that there are three divisions almost equal in amount to the whole Bombay army under the charge of one Major-General, viz.:—

Presidency	17,308
Cawnpur	11,798
Meerut	16,551

This arrangement was caused by a different order of things when the Bombay Presidency was disconnected with the others, and when separate establishments were indispensable to its efficiency. The necessity no longer exists, and it seems practicable to substitute for it another which will save a very great charge, and will, I venture to think, not be unacceptable to all the individuals concerned.

I would propose that the Bombay army as such should be at once abolished, the Hindustáni half of it being transferred in complete regiments to the Bengal army, the Bombay half[1] to remain as a separate corps to be recruited always within the territories; to be commanded by a Major-General with the same staff as any other division of the army, and the commissariat and ordnance departments being incorporated with those of Bengal or Madras as may be convenient. I am of course supposing the previous adoption of the general equalisation of all allowances.

To the officers I conceive that the larger field of employment and the superior healthiness of many of the stations in the Upper Provinces would be agreeable. To the men it would be much more satisfactory to be brought nearer their homes, and to be saved the danger of the long journey which has been so fatal to many when returning on furlough. The State, besides the saving from the reduction of the staff, would make a great gain in the comparative cheapness of all camp establishments, of followers, &c. It is an extraordinary fact not yet accounted for that in all the stations occupied alternately by Madras, Bombay, and Bengal troops, the Bazaar prices have invariably fallen with the last and risen with the two former.

The Bombay division would under this alteration occupy only the stations within their frontier, transferring the southern Maráthá country to Madras, Nágpur[2] and Dísa to Bengal.

In considering the question of internal danger those officers most conversant with India affairs who were examined before the Parliamentary Committee apprehend no danger to our dominion as long as we are assured of the fidelity of our

[1] As this separate corps would be liable to degenerate into a sort of militia it might perhaps be a better arrangement to incorporate the Bombay half in the Madras army, in the same manner as the Hindustáni half would be drafted into that of Bengal.

[2] The following table of distances shows that Nágpur is as conveniently placed for support from three of the great military

native troops. To this opinion I entirely subscribe. But others again view in the native army itself the source of our greatest peril. In all ages the military body has been often the prime cause, but generally the instrument, of all revolutions; and proverbial almost as is the fidelity of the native soldier to the chief whom he serves, more especially when he is justly and kindly treated, still we cannot be blind to the fact that many of those ties which bind other armies to their allegiance are totally wanting in this. Here is no patriotism, no community of feeling as to religion or birthplace, no influencing attachment from high considerations, or great honours and rewards. Our native army also is extremely ignorant, capable of the strongest religious excitement, and very sensitive to disrespect to their persons or infringement of their customs.

I shall quote from the evidence a few of those passages bearing upon this subject which appear to me to have the greatest force and truth. Mr. Henry Russell observes:—

'The greatest danger we have to apprehend is from our native army; our military force is the exclusive tenure by which we hold the government, and the fidelity of the troops of whom that force is composed is necessarily precarious. They are foreigners and mercenaries. They are attached to a Government that pays them well and treats them kindly, &c., but we have no hold upon them through either national honour or national prejudices, and cannot expect from them what we do from English soldiers fighting for English objects. They are peculiarly susceptible of being practised

---

stations in Bengal as from Bombay, and much nearer to the divisions in Málwá and Ságar than even to Bombay:—

Nágpur to	Miles.	Nágpur to	Miles.
Bombay	560	Ságar (c)	181
Madras	735	Benares	446
Mhow (a)	351	Allahábád	450
Nímach (b)	505	Agra	669

(a) Left cantonment of the Rájputána force.
(b) Centre of the Rájputána force.
(c) Head-quarters of Ságar division.

upon, and may be induced either by our own mismanagement or by the artifices of designing persons to turn against us those very arms which now constitute our only strength.'

This intelligent officer makes a remark too true at the present day with respect to the Madras army :—

'The details of the army had for the first time in India fallen into the hands of a school which thought that everything depended on show, and that no sacrifice was too great for the attainment of outward smartness and uniformity.'

There are parts of Mr. Holt Mackenzie's evidence well worthy of attention, for no man of his time in India possessed the same general knowledge or could form a more accurate and enlightened judgment upon all subjects connected with our rule. He observes: 'I do not think the sepoys have any attachment to the English as a nation; on the contrary, I apprehend that a considerable number of that part which consists of Moslems must generally have a national, or rather I should say a religious, dislike to the English.' He thinks 'the sepoys have a great deal of attachment to their officers, but that this rests upon personal character rather than on anything that may be called attachment to the nation generally.' He thinks 'the sepoys, as long as they are well paid, will have so strong a sense of the duty of being faithful to those who so pay them as to be only overcome by some powerful cause of discontent or excitement.' He thinks a larger native army is quite essential for maintaining the tranquillity of the country, but he would be 'very sorry to see its defence entrusted to them without a large European force.' He is not aware of any circumstances causing immediate danger, but he thinks 'on general principles that there is much prospective danger.'

It is only since I recorded different minutes enforcing the precedence and expediency of bettering the condition of the native army and of preventing discontent by timely concession and precaution that I have read a passage in a letter from Sir Thomas Munro, written in 1817, in which I find a view of our future situation and the consequences appertaining to it quite in unison with the sentiments I have so often expressed. He observes: 'But even if all India could be brought under the British dominion, it is very questionable whether such a change, either as it regards the natives or ourselves, ought to be desired. One effect of such a conquest would be that the Indian army, having no longer any warlike neighbours to control, would gradually lose its military habits and discipline, and that the native troops would have leisure to feel their own strength, and, for want of other employment, to turn it against their European masters.' He concludes a long and able argument upon the question whether in the event of our conquest of the whole of India the condition of the people would be better than under their native princes, which he doubts, with this remark: 'There is perhaps no example of any conquest in which the natives have been so completely excluded from all share in the government of their country as in British India.' The only conclusion that I wish to establish from the preceding remarks, which contain indisputable truths, is that in the native army alone rests our internal danger, and that this danger may involve our complete subversion. But the fidelity of our native army, though wonderfully great and deserving of high confidence, cannot be considered exempt from the possibility of seduction, and thus an adequate European force is the sole security against this, the greatest evil that could befall us. What should be the proportion of our European to our native force will be presently considered.

The external danger comes next under review. The capability of the native army to meet it, and the manner in which the native military means of India can be turned to the greatest advantage, are subjects of the first magnitude.

As far as experience can teach us, the prospect is discouraging as to any great degree of direct and positive assistance in the field, that is in actual conflict, to be expected from the sepoy in a contest with the stronger and bolder races of Central Asia, with or without the co-operation of a Russian force. Mr. Holt Mackenzie has given an opinion upon the question before us, which quite coincides with my view of it :—

'My impression is that as far as regards any Indian enemy the native army may be considered to be very efficient. I am not equally confident of this efficiency if placed in any new and unusual position and exposed to encounter enemies that may possibly come upon us from without. I think the result of the war with the Burmese seems to show that when brought against enemies superior in physical strength to those with whom they have been accustomed to contend, and required to surmount obstacles of a different kind from what they have been accustomed to surmount, the native troops, however well led, will be found to want resolution and nervous vigour so as to be inferior to European troops in a degree not ordinarily to be perceived in Indian warfare. Consequently I should apprehend that if they were called upon to meet an European enemy in the north of India they might fail partly from the want of physical strength and partly from the want of moral energy.'

The defects of the native of India are a want of physical strength and of moral energy. The first is beyond our remedy. It only depends upon ourselves to raise the latter to a much higher standard. Our system has, I fear, tended to depress it.

The late wars have brought the sepoy in contact with enemies of masculine character, and have shown the justice of the preceding opinion.

Sir David Ochterlony, in his confidential report to Government during the Nepál war, has recorded his opinion that the sepoys were unequal to contend with the Gúrkhas in the hills.

The Burmese war was exclusively carried on by British troops. The Madras troops entirely failed. It is understood that Sir Archibald Campbell was strongly prejudiced against them, and when granting the request of their officers to be permitted to lead their men to the attack, he neglected the practice invariably adopted upon all other occasions of joining with them a proportion of European troops To this their ill-success may be in part owing. My own impression is also that in the short war against Coorg the Madras sepoys showed the same want of energy.

With respect to the inability of the sepoys to contend with a European enemy, the concurrent opinion of all the evidence, to which may be added the inference to be drawn from all our own conquests in India, seems to be decisive upon the question.

For my own part I am not quite disposed to come to the same desponding conclusion, because if the bolder and larger man of the north were mixed with a due proportion of European troops, and excited to acts of valour by sufficient encouragement, I know not why he should not acquire the same superior bearing as the Portuguese and the Neapolitans under British and French direction. But of the sepoys of the south of India, of those of the territories proper of Madras and Bombay, I entertain no such hope. Their case cannot be more favourably put for them than by supposing them to be Europeans, and to have all the advantages of the European character, and then let it be asked if men of such physical inferiority would be received as recruits in any European army, or if an army so constituted would not be considered perfectly inefficient.

All these facts and opinions seem to me to establish incontrovertibly that a large proportion of European troops is necessary for our security under all circumstances of peace and war. It surprises me to find how little attention was paid by the Committee to one of the most important parts of the inquiry, the relative proportions between the native and European force. But we fortunately possess the opinion of Sir Thomas Munro, the first of authorities, confirmed by another only second to his, that of Colonel John Munro, who filled the office of Quartermaster-General when I was at Madras. The opinions on both these questions are worthy of being noticed.

'The native troops are in an excellent state of discipline, but of course the Europeans are always superior to the natives. Question is, What should be the relative proportions of the European infantry to the native infantry? Answer: I should say one-third of European; that was the proportion observed at Madras,—indeed we have sometimes rather more, now we have considerably less.'

I once conversed with Sir Thomas Munro on that point, and he expressed his opinion very decidedly that there should be that proportion. This is also my own opinion, but I think that it would suffice at present to fix it at one-fourth, being careful that the establishment should be always kept complete, and that on the most remote indications of danger it should be increased to one-third.

The statements annexed to this Minute show the actual proportion of Europeans to natives in the army of each presidency, and in the whole army.

The raising the European proportion to one-fourth would require an establishment of 28,171 rank and file. The present establishment of King's troops consists of twenty regiments of infantry and four of cavalry. The numbers wanting to complete amount to 1945 rank and file, and the effective strength consists only of 15,587 rank and file. The three European regiments in the Company's service amount to 2429 rank and file. They exceed their complement. The total effective force, both King's and Company's, amounts to 18,016 rank and file, and the deficit required to complete the whole to one-fourth would be 10,155 rank and file, of which 8599 would be in excess of the present establishment, supposing the King's regiments to be complete and the Company's European corps reduced to their complement. In order to maintain the proportion of one-fourth in a state of efficiency, it is necessary to advert to the very great difference there is, and must always be, between the apparent and the real force, that is between the number of men actually borne on the rolls, and those if the regiment took the field who would be forthcoming. Many from the effects of climate must be left behind in hospital and quarters.

I called on Dr. Burke, the Inspector-General of Hospitals, an officer of great experience and intelligence, for an opinion of the deductions that ought to be made on this score. His answer gives 8 per cent. for sick left behind and 4 per cent. more for the effects of even a long march on a very short service. In order to keep up this one-fourth to its proper quota I think the establishment of rank and file should be fixed at 25,000 infantry and 5000 cavalry, and to effect it at the least possible charge I would raise each of our twenty-three regiments of infantry to 1000 rank and file, and add to our establishment two regiments of King's infantry. The cavalry, as I have already proposed in a former minute, should be raised to 800 rank and file, and the establishment augmented from three to five regiments, being 1000 men short of the force proposed.

I would station these two additional regiments of infantry and two of cavalry as follows—one of infantry at Bangalore, making three regiments at that station, which I consider as the most convenient position for a reserve, to be applicable to all exigencies in India; one regiment of infantry and one of cavalry to be placed in the great centrical cantonment, Rájputána, proposed to be established on the Beas river, and the other regiment of cavalry at Haiderábád.

In Rájputána there are above 10,000 native troops without any European force, which I consider to be highly objectionable in many points of view. This tract of country between the Narbadá and Jumna, or rather between Nágpur and Agra, is by far the most important in the whole line of our military occupation.

I do not feel called upon to suggest the means by which this extra expense shall be defrayed. My duty is performed in stating the imperfections of our present military defence and the measures that are necessary for the security of our empire. At the same time it appears to me that the reduction of one captain in every regiment of native infantry and cavalry may be made without any compromise of efficiency. When two companies were reduced in each regiment the former complement of officers remained unaltered. I consider the establishment of European officers in a native regiment to be far more than is necessary, and it is their number and high pay which swell to such an immense amount the military expenditure. Men differ very much as to the proper proportion, some contending that the amount cannot be too great; others, again, that the sepoy army was never in a better state than when there were not more than three or four officers with each corps. I am much inclined to be of this opinion. The connection between European and native officers was much closer, their dependence upon each other greater, and a more cordial intimacy existed between all ranks. I believe the sepoys have never been so good as they were in the earliest part of our career; none superior to those under De Boigne, and at the present day none better than the Nizam's contingent, where the same proportion, I believe, about six officers, is maintained. There is one fact that is universally admitted, that no number of European officers will make a sepoy corps equal to an European regiment, and in my opinion that establishment would be sufficient that allowed the presence of one officer to a company. The saving proposed would go far to meet the charge, in addition to the changes that have been suggested in respect to the Bombay army.

There are two points adverted to in the reports of the Committee that are well deserving of early consideration.

Both the Madras Committee and the Adjutant-General

and Quartermaster-General of the Bengal army have recommended the augmentation of each native centre to 1000 men, without any increase of officers, and I would strongly support its adoption as soon as the finances will allow. It would give great relief to the duty devolving upon all sepoy corps, which is often very harassing and distressing as military duty, and increased by the interference and interruption often caused to their religious customs. This increase would permit the extension of a much valued indulgence, that of furlough, to a much larger proportion of every regiment—say one-fifth, and for a longer period—say a year. I should think it would in any new general regulation be advisable to reduce the amount of pay received during absence. There is at this time a great difference of practice in this respect between the Bengal sepoys and those of Madras and Bombay, to the advantage of the latter.

The same Bengal officers have urged the formation of a portion of the regular regiments into light infantry. As there is not a single chief in India or on the frontier who can resist us in line, an army formed principally for that purpose is in a great degree useless. Within our territories all insurrection must be confined to hills or the jungles. Without we have either the Nepál Hills or the jungles and stockades of Ava, where soldiers well trained in irregular fighting and in the expert use of a light musket can alone be useful. I am of opinion that one cause of the defeat of the two columns in the late Coorg war may be ascribed to the ignorance of both men and officers in this species of warfare, which requires a particular and constant instruction as well as experience.

The irregular cavalry is the arm of all others in India that may be placed on a par with any of the military means that we could command for our defence against foreign invasion—not even excepting the European cavalry. I need not repeat what has been so often stated, that the Rohillas and all the other highest caste and bravest men in India who will not enter our ranks from dislike to our rigid discipline, and from the fear of personal disrespect from our young inconsiderate officers, have no repugnance to serve in the irregular cavalry. The irregular cavalry is of peculiar importance in India. It is the favourite arm of the native. It attaches him to our service by the strong ties of interest and affection. It prevents his being engaged against us, and if the system were sufficiently extended it would, at a trifling expense, afford us all the advantages, moral and military, which the Russians have derived from the Cossacks, who, from being the bitterest enemies of Russia in the time of Peter the Great, have become the most faithful subjects of the empire. This force should be increased to 20,000 men.

Steam power must be included among the most powerful means of reducing the difficulties of protection and support to such extensive and distant lines of defence and of multiplying the military resources that we already possess. In illustration of the practical use that might be made of this power, I take the liberty of introducing here an opinion that I have elsewhere expressed :—

'But an efficient marine steam establishment in India is called for by considerations more powerful even than those of commercial advantage or improved political control. It would multiply in a ratio little understood the defensive means of the Empire. Let me advert to an event, the particulars of which are within your recollection, the Burmese war. If five powerful steamers had then been at our command to bring up in quick succession all necessary rèinforcements and supplies, the war would probably have terminated in a few months, and many millions of treasure, many thousands of lives, and extraordinary misery and sickness would have been spared. Allow me to submit another estimate of advantage, of the correctness of which you all can likewise judge. The proper station for the principal reserve of our European troops in India is at Bangalore, Madras the place of embarkation. In a few days, at any period of the monsoons, the same five steamers would carry this force to the most distant part of the shores of the Empire. In five weeks with the aid of the river-steamers this reserve would reach Allahabad, the most centrical point of our territories, and one of our most commanding positions. The same steam power that would enable us to baffle any invader in war would be ample in times of peace to carry into complete execution the whole plan of the Bengal Steam Committee, for which I continue to be a decided advocate.'

I will only offer a remark that if such power be provided it should be exclusively appropriated to the transport of troops and to the maintenance of the communication with Europe. From all purposes of less utility—as passage or tug vessels—it should be interdicted as being uselessly expensive, and as affecting without any adequate return of benefit the efficiency and readiness for constant service of the steam machinery.

I shall only now take the liberty of suggesting the advantage that would accrue from including the military establishments of Ceylon in those entertained for the defence of our Indian Empire. Ceylon could well spare one regiment of infantry, which would be *pro tanto* a relief to her finances. For the ordinary duties of the colony a sepoy corps at one half of the expense would probably answer every purpose, and in case of more urgent service the regiment at Trichinopoli might be held at the disposal of the Government of Ceylon, and would be able to cross the straits in a very short time. The Ceylon regiment, if stationed at Bangalore, would be of much more extended benefit, could march down to replace the Trichinopoli regiment if necessary, and could move on to Ceylon in case of increasing urgency. There is a Malay corps in Ceylon, an element of defence not known in our Indian establishment, and which might be most usefully employed in our provinces on the Eastern coast, and perhaps in the Lower Provinces, which are so hateful to the up-country sepoy. If the experiment succeeded, this corps would afford a nucleus for the foundation of a larger force. It is a great desideratum in our military arrangements, the obtaining a mode of defence for Bengal proper at once efficient for the State and satisfactory to the individuals employed. I had much conversation with Sir Edward Barnes on the subject. I possess, indeed, a written memorandum from him strongly concurring in the view here taken, but I cannot inmediately lay my hand upon it.

I regret that these observations should have run to such extreme length, but no one before me has had the opportunity of a season of peace to reflect upon the alterations that the union of our Presidencies into one Government, and of our territories into one Empire, imperatively call for. It would have ill become me, upon a subject so momentous as the safety of this great possession, to have been prevented by any motive of delicacy from the full development of my opinion. I fearlessly pronounce the Indian army to be the least efficient and most expensive in the world. The realisation of the hypothesis with which I started, of the presence of 20,000 Russian infantry on the Indus, with its accompanying multitudes, would now find us in a state utterly unable to resist them. The national resources at home might possibly rescue us from the impending ruin, but we must recollect that we are not likely to have again the same large armies to supply us with great reinforcements, and that men recruited for the occasion would be very inefficient and quite inadequate to bear the effects of the climate.

But even if we could command this aid, it would be utterly inexcusable if, with ample time for preparation, with the sum of ten millions sterling appropriated to our military establishments, we were not able to secure ourselves against every calculable danger.

W. C. BENTINCK.

Calcutta, March 13th, 1835.

CHAPTER X

END OF INDIAN CAREER AND LIFE

THE Indian career of Lord William Bentinck has now been considered in all its bearings, and an attempt has been made to explain the influence he exercised over the development of British power in India. Considering that he had wielded authority in that country for a period of nearly seven years under circumstances of great anxiety, it is not surprising to find that his health suffered during the last few months of his stay there, but we cannot suppose that this fact greatly shortened his tenure of power, which, with the exception of Lord Hastings and Lord Dalhousie, was longer than that of any Governor-General in this century. His departure on 20th March, 1835, in the full height of his reputation, and when the task of reform in India had reached its end, not to be taken up for another generation, contrasted with the circumstances of his sudden and enforced exit from Madras in 1807. Even the sore feeling in the Services from his interference with what were regarded as cherished perquisites did not prevent their cordial expression of the opinion that he had done good work in India, and that his administration formed an epoch in the history of our government of the country. Among the natives the feeling of regret was naturally more acute, and found louder expression because in him they lost the friend and vindicator who, first among their English rulers, held out to them the prospect of equal rights and an honourable share in the government. Expression was given to their gratitude by the statue erected by public (and chiefly native) subscription to his memory, which forms a prominent ornament of the city of Calcutta, and which bears an inscription [1] prepared by his friend and coadjutor, Macaulay.

Lord William Bentinck went to India as a reformer, and he fully and honourably realised the character in which he was sent out by the East India Company.

[1] The following is the full text of this inscription :—

To
William Cavendish Bentinck,
who during seven years ruled India with eminent prudence,
integrity, and benevolence;
who, placed at the head of a great Empire, never laid aside the
simplicity and moderation of a private citizen;
who infused into Oriental despotism the spirit of British freedom;
who never forgot that the end of government is
the happiness of the governed;
who abolished cruel rites;
who effaced humiliating distinctions;
who gave liberty to the expression of public opinion;
whose constant study it was to elevate the intellectual and
moral character of the nation committed to his charge.
This Monument
was erected by men
who, differing in race, in manners, in language, and in religion,
cherish with equal veneration and gratitude
the memory of his wise, reforming, and paternal administration.

He began his work by placing the impaired finances of the Indian Government on a firm and satisfactory basis, not merely by converting a deficit into a surplus, but by effecting permanent economies and creating new sources of revenue. He carried out several great measures of reform which were necessary, not only in the interests of governed and governing, but also in order to demonstrate the earnest desire of the Company to consider the welfare of its subjects. He was the first to put in practice the loftier ideal of Indian government, which had insensibly grown up after the Warren Hastings trial.

If Lord William Bentinck had many admirers, it is not surprising, considering the acts of his administration, to find that he had also enemies and detractors. No one can forcibly reform the established order of things without incurring the enmity of those who are interfered with, and Lord William Bentinck certainly interfered with a good many people. Perhaps the writer who gave the most extreme expression to these injured feelings was Mr. Thornton in his History, concluding a long indictment of Bentinck's administration with an attack on his personal character, in which he said there was 'added the treachery of the Italian to the caution of the Dutchman[1].' But it is strange to find a writer like Greville, who was a shrewd judge of human character, and who was, moreover, Bentinck's own nephew, giving expression to what was

[1] A forcible and eloquent reply to Thornton's attack was published in the first volume of the *Calcutta Review*, and deserves to be read.

after all the antipathy to Lord William Bentinck felt by a very small class in India. We may assume that it was rather prejudice caused by his home politics, than objection to Bentinck's work in India, that led him to pen the following lines as his summing up of the character of his uncle:—

> 'He is a man whose success in life has been greater than his talents warrant, for he is not right-headed, and has committed some great blunder or other in every public situation in which he has been placed, but he is simple in his habits, popular in his manners, liberal in his opinions, and magnificently hospitable in his mode of life. These qualities are enough to ensure popularity.'

The most unfriendly critics of Lord William Bentinck have not ventured to deny that he accomplished the work entrusted to him, and that he satisfactorily solved the problems which came before him. Their criticism is not directed against the manner of the worker, but against the work itself. The decision to diminish the expense of government, to give the governed a larger share in it, and to elevate it for the benefit of the millions in India and the English reputation, was come to because those steps could be no longer put off. They originated not with Lord William Bentinck so much as in England under the pressure of an aroused, if still sluggish, public opinion, and if they had not been carried out by an officer of the East India Company, the neglect would have entailed the speedier fall of that institution and the transfer of its duties to the British Crown and Parliament.

But there is no justification for the loose statement so frequently made that the object of Lord William Bentinck was to facilitate the transfer of the government from English to native hands. He saw clearly, and long before he was Governor-General, that the administrative services would have to be recruited from the natives, and he recognised on principle the justice of this measure. He carried out what he approved, and what the Company itself saw to be necessary, in an expeditious and practical manner that provided an enduring and satisfactory remedy for the difficulty. Every subsequent step taken by the Government of India in the extension of the branches open to the natives of the country has been the direct consequence of Lord William Bentinck's policy. We have been told very often that this was a misfortune rather than a benefit, and that by so doing the seeds were planted of our overthrow. The prediction may be verified at some remote date, as to which no one but a rash prophet will attempt now to vaticinate.

But what would have been the stability of the English position in India if we had persisted in governing the country with a mere handful of our own officials, excluding the native from all superior administrative work, and either augmenting our expenses or diminishing our revenue in accordance as we kept many or few European officials? It would be going too far to assert that to-day there would not be a British India at all. We content ourselves by saying that it would be a British India of which we should have less reason to be proud than of that which exists, and also that it would be less secure.

Very little consideration was necessary to prove to thoughtful persons that two hundred millions of people, composed of many highly intelligent and spirited races, could not be kept permanently in a state of subjection without either voice or share in their own government. There is no instance in history of any race of capable conquerors having attempted so hopeless a task, and all Lord William Bentinck did was to prove that the Company, having thrown aside its commercial character, was prepared to discharge its duties as a purely governing body in a worthy manner. It was impossible to accomplish this task without giving umbrage to influential classes, and the completeness of Lord William Bentinck's success was certainly calculated to embitter the feeling against him among the old servants of the Company. But the allegation that his policy was calculated to undermine British power in India is one that will not bear examination.

It was indispensable. By enabling the revenues of India to meet all the charges of a foreign government he added to the strength and durability of our position in India, and his anxiety to augment our military forces in the country, and to oppose a Russian advance on India with a suitable foreign policy, showed that he would be no party to anything tending to weaken our hold upon the country. The more carefully Lord William Bentinck's Indian career is considered, the more evident will it appear that his part in consolidating British authority in India was a great and honourable one. To him we feel it to be due that the peoples of India were first convinced that a main factor in our policy was a disinterested desire for their own welfare.

The closing years of Lord William Bentinck's life, which was not long extended after the termination of his Indian administration, only call for brief notice. After his return to England in the autumn of 1835 he was offered a peerage, which he declined, partly because he had no children to inherit a title, and partly because he wished to return to active political life in the House of Commons. In the election of 1837 he was elected Member for the city of Glasgow in the Liberal interest. He spent a good deal of his time in France, where his Palermo friend of more than twenty years before had become Louis Philippe, King of the French, and he died at Paris on June 17, 1839, at the age of 65. The part of his life-work which will endure was performed in India, and although to him fell less of the pomp and circumstance of war which has formed so prominent a feature of our history in that country, and more of unattractive internal reform, he can never be excluded from the list of eminent rulers who made India a British possession, and who have kept it so, as much by the tacit assent of the subject population as by superior force.

INDEX

INDEX

THE END.